The Abbess of Andalusia

FLANNERY O'CONNOR'S SPIRITUAL JOURNEY

The *Abbess of* *Andalusia*

FLANNERY O'CONNOR'S *SPIRITUAL JOURNEY*

By
Lorraine V. Murray

SAINT BENEDICT PRESS, LLC
Charlotte, North Carolina
2009

To Monsignor Richard J. Lopez and
the Dominican Sisters of Hawthorne

And in memory of Mary Ann Long

" *N*ow Flannery is dead and I will write her name with honor, with love for the great slashing innocence of that dry-eyed irony that could keep looking at the South in the face without bleeding or even sobbing."

—*Thomas Merton*

CONTENTS

Acknowledgments

The idea for this book was born the moment that Monsignor Richard Lopez, my dear friend, turned to me one afternoon, as we sat sipping wine on the back porch, and inquired: "Have you ever read Flannery's letters?" His devotion and admiration for Flannery O'Connor kept me going over the next few years, as I read not only the letters, but a mountain of research material. He has my deepest gratitude.

I am also very grateful to Todd Aglialoro of Saint Benedict Press for his astute insights and superb editorial work on the manuscript.

Also high on my thank-you list are Ben Camardi of the Mary Flannery O'Connor Charitable Trust for kindly granting me permission to quote from Flannery's unpublished letters; Craig Amason, executive director of Andalusia and the Flannery O'Connor-Andalusia Foundation, for giving my husband and me a tour of Andalusia, and then answering my numerous questions via e-mail; and Joseph Pearce and Paul Thigpen, who gave me excellent guidance on an earlier draft of the book.

Along the way, I have made some new e-mail friends, and one is Bill Sessions, who knew Flannery and her mother very well, and was always gracious about replying to my questions. There were also folks in the Flannery O'Connor Society who encouraged me, especially Avis Hewitt, Bruce Gentry, Robert Donahoo, and Susan Presley.

A number of priests, sisters, and brothers came to my rescue, and I can never repay their kindnesses. They include the Dominican Sisters of Hawthorne, especially Mother Ann Marie at the Rosary Hill Home in Hawthorne, N.Y., who wrote a lovely letter containing memories about Sister Evangelist, and Sister Mary De Paul, who sent me letters from the archives.

Father Edward J. Romagosa wrote me a letter about his memories of Flannery, while Brother Chaminade Crabtree and Father Luke Kot at the Monastery of the Holy Spirit in Conyers sent information about Flannery and her peacocks. My cousin Father Christopher Viscardi helped me locate materials in the Jesuit house in Spring Hill, Alabama.

Librarians are the unsung angels that make many books possible, and this one is no exception. My appreciation goes to: Nancy Davis Bray in the Special Collections Room at Georgia College and State University in Milledgeville for helping me get information about Flannery's prayer book; Joan E. Gaulene at the New Orleans Province Jesuit Archives in the Monroe Library at Loyola University, for her help with a cache of letters to Father Youree Watson; Michael Carter at the Cloisters, Metropolitan Museum of Art, New York, for assistance in locating the laughing Madonna and Christ Child image.

I also thank Stephen Enniss, Naomi Nelson, Kathy Shoemaker, and Teresa Burk at the Manuscripts,

Archives, and Rare Book Library at Emory University for their assistance with Flannery's unpublished letters to Betty Hester; Janie Morris and David Strader at the Rare Book, Manuscript, and Special Collections Library at Duke University for help obtaining copies of unpublished letters to Father McCown; and Tracy Powell and Pat Ziebart at the Pitts Theology Library at Emory University for cheerfully helping me find magazine articles.

Special thanks go to the interlibrary loan specialist in the Pitts Theology Library – my husband, Jef Murray – for getting me a copy of the exact edition of the prayer book that Flannery used. He also made excellent suggestions on an early draft, fed me delicious meals and homemade wine, and encouraged me when the footnotes threatened to overwhelm me.

I also very much appreciate Dr. M. Patrick Graham, director of the Pitts Theology Library, for approving the purchase of books necessary for my research, and Dr. John Weaver and my other colleagues for their interest in the project.

I thank everyone who prayed for me as I wrote this book, especially my sister and brother-in-law, Rosemary and Dick Mende, my nieces, Christina Edgar and Jennifer Metcalf, my nephew, Rick Mende, my aunt, Rita Pope, my best friend, Pam Mottram, and my cousin Julie Anderson. I'm also grateful for prayers offered by the Dominican Sisters of Hawthorne, the brothers at the Monastery of the Holy Spirit, Mary Anne Castranio and Gretchen Keiser at *The Georgia Bulletin,* and my faith community at St. Thomas More Church in Decatur, Georgia.

PREFACE

One of the most memorable characters to emerge from the gargoylesque pen of Flannery O'Connor is The Misfit in "A Good Man Is Hard to Find." He is savagely psychopathic and yet, at the same time, savagely sane. "I call myself The Misfit," he said, "because I can't make what all I done wrong fit what all I gone through in punishment." In perceiving himself as a hapless victim of injustice, he appears to be a kindred spirit with that other "madman," King Lear, who declared himself "a man more sinn'd against than sinning."

The problem with which The Misfit struggles, in his case unsuccessfully, is the conundrum at the heart of life itself. Why do we suffer, and are we more sinned against than sinning? This was the conundrum at the very crux of G.K. Chesterton's novel *The Man Who Was Thursday*, which explores the mind's quest for meaning in the face of seemingly meaningless suffering. At the novel's end, the mysterious figure of Sunday emerges as a figure of the Divine, accused of inflicting so much apparently senseless pain. He is asked, "Have you ever suffered?" to which he replies with the words of Christ: "Can ye drink of the cup that I drink of?"

Although Sunday answers the question with another question, his question *is* the answer. It is the suffering of God Himself that makes sense of all suffering, and it is through Christ's suffering that Christians find meaning and purpose in their own. This axiomatic truth is at the sacred heart of the Christian's *acceptance* of suffering, an acceptance which Chesterton's friend, Maurice Baring, conveyed with sublime eloquence through the words of a character in *Darby and Joan*, the final novel he wrote before his own slow and painful death from Parkinson's disease:

"One has to *accept* sorrow for it to be of any healing power, and that is the most difficult thing in the world . . . A Priest once said to me, 'When you understand what *accepted* sorrow means, you will understand everything. It is the secret of life.'"[1]

This secret of life had been discovered by Fyodor Dostoevsky, who believed that his life had been positively transformed by his sufferings as a prisoner: "It was a good school. It strengthened my faith and awakened my love for those who bear all their suffering with patience."[2] Dostoevsky's great literary compatriot, Alexander Solzhenitsyn, underwent a similar transformation through his experience in the Gulag and, most particularly, through his near-death experience with cancer. By any stretch of the imagination, Solzhenitsyn's real-life experience of suffering at the hands of unjust jailers eclipses any injustice that we can imagine was suffered by The Misfit, yet, unlike The Misfit, Solzhenitsyn not only accepted his suffering but was grateful for its healing qualities.

"Years go by, yes," Solzhenitsyn wrote to his wife from Ekibastuz labor camp, "but if the heart grows warmer from the misfortunes suffered, if it is cleansed therein – the years are not going by in vain."[3]

The paradox is that suffering is not meaningless, as is claimed by Chesterton's satanic accuser and the manically rational Misfit, but that, on the contrary, it uncovers the secret at the heart of life. Far from being senseless, it actually makes sense of ourselves and our place in the cosmos. It is not needless but necessary.

Flannery O'Connor knew and embraced all of this. Her experience of suffering, and the strengthening of faith and awakening of love that it heralded, is manifested in her work; indeed it could even be said to have been *incarnated* in her work, the pain serving as her Muse. "I have been through a lot and will see and experience even more – you shall see how much I will have to write about."[4] Dostoevsky's words could as easily have been O'Connor's.

In "A Good Man Is Hard to Find" the real absence of this acceptance, as revealed by The Misfit's complaints about the suffering that he had experienced, leads to a desire to inflict suffering on others. The anger that is the bitter fruit of The Misfit's non-acceptance is literally deadly, and, significantly, is rooted in theology, not psychology. His non-acceptance of suffering is a consequence of his non-acceptance of Christ's Death and Resurrection:

"Jesus was the only One that ever raised the dead... and He shouldn't have done it. He thrown everything off balance. If He did what He said, then it's nothing for you to do but throw away everything and follow Him, and if He didn't, then it's nothing for you to do but enjoy the few minutes you got left the best way you can – by killing somebody or burning down his house or doing some other meanness to him. No pleasure but meanness," he said and his voice had become almost a snarl.

Solzhenitsyn lamented that the hedonistic modern world considered the acceptance of suffering as "masochism,"[5] yet here, in O'Connor's story, we see that the absence of such acceptance leads to sadism, and sadism of the most psychotic kind.

The brilliance of O'Connor's use of the grotesque is that her stories bring the essential metaphysics to the surface. She presents us with gargoyles, such as The Misfit and joyless Hulga, in order to show us the face of the devil. Her grotesque conceits unmask the devil, to borrow the title of Regis Martin's excellent study of O'Connor,[6] by removing the mask of the mundane that obscures the struggle of good and evil at the heart of reality. It's as if she picks up the stone with which we've hardened our hearts in order to reveal the nest of cockroaches, or serpents, lurking beneath.

"My subject in fiction is the action of grace in territory held largely by the devil," she tells us,[7] echoing the words of Dostoevsky in *The Brothers Karamazov*: "The awful thing is that beauty is mysterious as well as terrible. God and the devil are fighting there, and the battlefield is the heart of man."[8] This is the battlefield of which O'Connor writes, and it's the most realistic battlefield of all because it's the one on which we're all fighting, whether we like it or not, or indeed even know it.

✠   ✠   ✠   ✠

Flannery O'Connor is one of the brightest gems in the priceless crown of the Catholic Literary Revival. "The Catholic novel," she insisted, "is not necessarily about a Christianized or Catholicized world, but one in which the truth as Christians know it has been used

as a light to see the world by."⁹ According to this definition, she is herself a Catholic novelist par excellence.
She knows that her readers will only begin to see the
beauty of a life with Christ by seeing the ugliness of
a world without Him. She shows us the value of the
light by showing us the darkness, reminding us that
we do not value the good things in our lives until we
lose them.

"There is a moment in every great story," O'Connor
tells us, "in which the presence of grace can be felt as it
waits to be accepted or rejected, even though the reader
may not recognize this moment."¹⁰ The presence of grace
can be felt on almost every page of the present volume, in
which Lorraine V. Murray guides us through the spiritual
life of the inestimable Miss O'Connor – who was herself
a misfit, though of a very different ilk from the one in her
story. She was a misfit in the sense that we are all misfits, which is to say, in the wonderful words of the *Salve
Regina,* that she is a poor banished child of Eve, an exile
in this vale of tears, a sojourner, a stranger in a strange
land.

Yet she was more of a misfit than most. As a Georgian,
she was a misfit in a Yankee-dominated world; and as
a cradle Catholic in the staunchly Protestant and alien-
ated South, she was a misfit among misfits. She was an
outsider looking in to a world in which she did not really
belong, and yet, gift of gifts, she could see that world from
the inside and show that world itself in new and startling
ways. In short, she saw clearly because she saw through
the eyes of the Church. In this book, Lorraine V. Murray,
author of the edifying and inspiring *Confessions of an
Ex-Feminist,* allows us to see through the edifying and
inspirational eyes of Flannery O'Connor. In doing so, we

will see through the eyes of the Church Herself all the more clearly.

Joseph Pearce

Joseph Pearce is associate professor of literature and writer-in-residence at Ave Maria University in Florida. He is the author of many books, including biographies of Shakespeare, Chesterton, Tolkien, C. S. Lewis, and Oscar Wilde, and is editor of the Saint Austin Review *(www.staustinreview.com).*

INTRODUCTION

Afternoon at Andalusia

It's a blistering summer day as my husband and I head to Andalusia, the Georgia farm where Flannery O'Connor lived for thirteen years until her death at age thirty-nine. We leave the downtown area of Milledgeville and drive by a tacky strip of stores and fast-food restaurants, which in Flannery's day would have been fields and pasture. Across the street from a car dealership, we spot the small sign marked "Andalusia" and make a turn into the driveway. The entrance to Andalusia is protected by a gate, which has been unlocked for visitors today, and we drive down a single-lane dirt road.

Our first impression is of delicious solitude and silence, although I recall from Flannery's letters that in her day there would have been the piercingly loud cries of her peacocks, especially at night. "Lee-yon, lee-yon, mee-yon, mee-yon! Eee-e-yoy, eee-e-yoy!" they would call, according to her own description.

We park the car near a falling-down barn and mosey over toward the house, stopping briefly to peek at a mule that is completely engrossed in munching on some apparently delicious grasses. The animal ignores our pleas for attention and refuses to come nearer, but my husband manages to get a few photos.

We climb the steps leading into the two-story white farmhouse, where Flannery wrote her novels and short stories as well as hundreds of letters to friends, and received guests. We join a small cluster of visitors fanning themselves in the entryway. There, Craig Amason, the executive director of Andalusia, is mentioning a few highlights about Flannery, who has been hailed as one of the greatest Southern writers of the twentieth century. As we listen, I imagine Flannery popping up behind him to tell the visitors that in her day, "We had no bookstore in Milledgeville, but we had the largest mental institution in the world."

The house is stifling, despite a weary window air-conditioner, laboring to provide some respite from the heat. As I break out in a head-to-toe sweat, I recall reading a letter in which Flannery told friends it was not the heat she minded, but the cold, especially when the pipes froze and left the household without water.

To the left of the stairway, there is a small, humble room with a narrow bed, a generous number of bookshelves, a desk, and a manual typewriter. Flannery's room – as no-frills as her letters described. I look in somewhat sheepishly, since Flannery was such a private person that she didn't even allow her spiritual advisor and good friend, Father James Hart McCown, to see her room. Once again I imagine Flannery poking her head out and making some appropriately outrageous remark, this time about people who go on pilgrimages to famous places, as she once did, albeit very reluctantly, to Lourdes.

The room reminds me a bit of a cell in a monastery, of which Flannery might be considered the abbess. She was a woman who didn't crave fancy trappings, who started each day with prayer. She knew she had just enough, and not much more, to do the one thing she had been put on earth to do: write. When she took a break, she'd look out the window near her desk and sometimes spot her mother shooing the peacocks away from the flowers, one of their favorite treats.

Flannery's crutches, displayed by the simple bed, provide a sense of the odd paradox of this woman's life. Her disease clearly placed limitations on her world, but those limitations meant a deeper devotion to writing and less time wasted on diversions. Her slow decline from lupus was from one point of view tragic, but from her Catholic perspective, it was something to be accepted with humor and grace. Her Catholic faith taught that Christ's sacrifice on the Cross had changed suffering forever, giving it a deeper meaning, and she lived as if she believed it. Yet if you were to openly admire the way she so graciously handled the gradual diminishments of her life, she would surely bristle. She hated being called holy, and she had no time for self-pity.

As we climb the steep stairway, we notice a framed illustration depicting the Sacred Heart of Jesus. It is a stunning reminder that the inhabitants of this Deep South farmhouse, located in a largely Protestant town, were solidly Catholic. In an upstairs room there is displayed a generously sized, framed print, "After Golgotha," showing the grief-stricken Blessed Virgin Mary being comforted by friends, with a Cross upon a hill in the distance.

Downstairs, we enter the kitchen, remarkably small by today's standards, and the dining room, remarkably large, with a long hardwood table that could easily sit a dozen people, bespeaking a household where guests were welcomed. You can almost hear the chatter of guests gathered at that table: people who once included Sister

Evangelist and other sisters from Our Lady of Perpetual Help Home in Atlanta, Abbot Augustine Moore and Father Paul Bourne from the Monastery of the Holy Spirit in Conyers, Georgia, and Father McCown.

We learn from Craig Amason that the mule, named Flossie, is a descendant of the burros that lived on the farm in Flannery's time. As we are leaving, we try calling the animal's name, which results in her ignoring us with greater determination. In some ways, Flossie is a more poignant reminder of Flannery than anything in the house, because the burros, along with ducks, chickens, and, of course, the famous peafowl, were Flannery's real delight, whereas the day-day-day running of the dairy farm and the household were left to her mother, Regina, with help from Flannery's uncle, Louis Cline.

That evening, we visit Sacred Heart Church in Milledgeville, where Flannery and Regina worshiped. There, in an outdoor garden, amidst clusters of hearty roses, we see a large, pure-white statue of the Virgin holding court. A plaque asks visitors to say a Hail Mary for the lady who long ago gave the statue to the church. Obediently, I clasp the outstretched hand of this stone Madonna and say two prayers: one for the lady and one, in gratitude and love, for God's gift of Flannery O'Connor.

✠   ✠   ✠   ✠

Who exactly was Flannery O'Connor? A friend once called her a saint, but she quickly insisted that he stop repeating such "slop." After her death, her spiritual director praised her as an "unappreciated prophet in her home town."[11] And just a few years ago, an author referred to her as a smart, Catholic writer who surely felt out of place there because, he avowed, Milledgeville, Georgia, was Protestant and deeply conservative.[12]

On the wall of a bed and breakfast in Milledgeville today there hangs a poster that would have piqued Flannery's interest. It promotes conferences sponsored by her nearby alma mater's Office of Multicultural Diversity, and among the topics probed and dissected by professors is one on Flannery O'Connor's fiction. That might not have surprised her, but the blurb appears just inches away from one about a play called *The Vagina Monologues* – and that surely would have caused her amusement. If she were alive today, it's easy to imagine her unleashing a few appropriately scathing remarks about that title and pointing out to friends the blinding light of the obvious: some words aren't fit to be used in polite company, even in the twenty-first century.

"*I Was Home*"

Would that opinion make her terribly out of place in today's world? Maybe in some circles, but certainly not the ones in which she was comfortable. She was smart, she was witty, she was deeply creative – and she was, above all, a faithful Catholic. She was the kind of Catholic who went to weekday Masses whenever she could. And when she entered a church where she knew none of the congregation and not a single priest, she was the kind of Catholic who would say, "As soon as I went in the door, I was home."[13]

Technically, of course, home for her was Milledgeville, which was, and is, Protestant and small. Still, it would be wrong to conclude that she felt out of place there. She was quite content to live in a two-story white house on a 544-acre dairy farm in a town she described, tongue-in-cheek, as a "Bird Sanctuary, where all is culture, graciousness, refinement, and bidnis-like common sense."[14] Although she left the South for five years, she later said her best writing had been done there after her return.[15] No fan of teeming cities, she put Atlanta first on her list of places to get away from, giving thanks to the Lord for being "a hermit novelist."[16]

Self-Portrait in Letters

There have been hundreds of articles and dozens of books written about the stories this hermit novelist created, and scores of articles penned about her life. However, in this book we will go on a different journey. We will not analyze her plot lines, parse her sentences, or flesh out the symbols in her stories. Instead, we will aim to uncover the self-portrait Flannery created in the daily stream of letters that poured out of Andalusia.

For in those letters, crafted with humor and wisdom and addressed to friends who were students and readers, fledgling writers, priests and nuns, Flannery created a spiritual autobiography of sorts. As her dear friend Sally Fitzgerald aptly noted, "The true likeness of Flannery O'Connor will be painted by herself, a self-portrait in words, to be found in her letters."[17]

These letters show a woman with a fierce sense of humor, and with strong opinions: on everything from the sad state of the Catholic press to the joys of raising peacocks. They also reveal a woman who was steadfast in her faith, even though she felt that she was writing for an audience that no longer believed in God. Indeed, she often was trounced by critics, who complained about the violence in her stories and would then, in their own bloodthirsty way, tear the tales "limb from limb."[18] However, she was quick to point out that her knowledge of violence certainly was not from firsthand experience, since she hailed from people who checked under the beds every night and found nothing.[19]

Catholic Roots

Mary Flannery O'Connor was born on March 25, 1925. It was the Feast of the Annunciation, celebrating the moment heralded by the archangel Gabriel, when the Word became flesh in the womb of the Blessed Virgin. Born in Savannah, she was the only child of her Roman Catholic parents, Regina Cline O'Connor and Edward Francis O'Connor, Jr. She was baptized in Savannah at the Cathedral of Saint John the Baptist,[20] which became the center of her sacramental life: it was there she made her First Communion in 1932 and was confirmed two years later.

Her family's Catholic roots in the Protestant South ran deep. Her maternal great-grandfather, Hugh Donnelly Treanor, born in Ireland, made history when he became Milledgeville's first Catholic resident in 1833. The very first Mass celebrated in Milledgeville took place in Mr. Treanor's hotel room, and after his home was built, a priest said Mass there using the piano as a makeshift altar.[21] Mrs. Hugh Donnelly Treanor later generously donated the land upon which Sacred Heart Catholic Church was built in 1874.[22] Another history-maker was Flannery's grandfather, Peter James Cline, who in 1888 was elected the first Catholic mayor of that same small, Protestant Georgia town.[23]

Ice Cream and Lilies

Little Mary Flannery's childhood was richly populated with nuns. When she was four, the family took her to visit a cousin who was the Mother Superior of a convent in Augusta. The sisters served ice cream in the shape of Calla lilies that day, and thinking that nuns ate that way every day, Flannery was tempted to join a religious order.[24]

At six, she enrolled at St. Vincent's Grammar School in Savannah, where the Irish Sisters of Mercy drilled her on the basic teachings in *The Baltimore Catechism*. It was there she created a lasting memory for one classmate by shooting the rubber bands off her braces when the nuns' backs were turned.[25]

At Sacred Heart School in Savannah, where Flannery transferred in 1936, she learned her lessons under the watchful eyes of the Sisters of St. Joseph of Carondolet. She also joined the Girl Scouts, although she was not that keen on hiking; she preferred to spend her spare time writing and drawing.[26] As the Depression deepened, her father's business began floundering. To make matters worse, he also was struggling with health problems. He would eventually be diagnosed with lupus erythematosus, an incurable autoimmune disorder.

In 1938, Mr. O'Connor took a job with the Federal Housing Administration in Atlanta, and the family moved to the city. It soon became apparent that mother and daughter were not at all keen on city life, so they re-located to the Cline family home in Milledgeville, while Mr. O'Connor remained in Atlanta, visiting the family on weekends. Flannery went to Peabody High School, where she wrote articles and drew cartoons for the school newspaper. As her father's health worsened, he quit his job and returned to Milledgeville, dying of lupus in 1941. It was a terrible blow for Flannery, who was then a month shy of her sixteenth birthday.[27]

Security in Mass

Flannery's accomplishments have been well-documented by her close friend Sally Fitzgerald. Most O'Connor fans know that she majored in social science at Georgia State College for Women in Milledgeville – now known as Georgia College and State University. She was called Flannery by friends, although relatives continued using her childhood name.[28] After graduation, honors came fast and furious, including a scholarship to the State University of Iowa, where she started out in journalism, but then enrolled in the Writers' Workshop. There, far from home, she found security in daily Mass at St. Mary's Church in Iowa City.

After receiving a Master of Fine Arts degree in 1947, she received an invitation to Yaddo, an artists' colony near Saratoga Springs, New York. There, her religion grounded her as it had in the Protestant South, and she attended Mass each day with the colony's domestic staff.[29] In 1949, she moved to New York City and lived in an apartment building on the corner of Broadway and West 108th street, going to daily Mass at nearby Ascension Church. She then re-located to a garage apartment behind a house owned by her Catholic friends Sally and Robert Fitzgerald in Ridgefield, Connecticut. On this wooded hilltop she continued working on her first novel, *Wise Blood,* which she'd begun in Iowa, and helped the Fitzgeralds care for their children. Shortly before Christmas in 1950, she boarded a train in Connecticut to visit her family in Georgia. It was then her life took a decidedly different direction.

Stalked by the Wolf

When Sally Fitzgerald took her to the station, she described Flannery as walking a bit stiffly, but otherwise fine. However, by the time Flannery arrived in Milledgeville, the situation had worsened considerably, and Flannery's uncle described her as resembling a "shriveled old woman." A few nights later, Regina called the Fitzgeralds to tell them the shocking news: the doctors said her daughter was dying of lupus, the same autoimmune disease that had claimed her father's life. [30]

Lupus takes its name from the Latin word for wolf, and it stalks its prey heartlessly, causing painful inflammation, swelling in the joints, fevers, rashes, fatigue, and eventual death. The wolf overcame Flannery abruptly, when she was just twenty-five, and over the next fourteen years the disease gradually diminished her mobility, sapped her energy, and increased her dependency on her mother. However, she rarely complained about the illness, seeming to accept it, for the most part, with equanimity and even humor. After the initial attack, she did not return to Connecticut, but instead moved with Regina to the family farm, called Andalusia. The rest, as they say, is history.

Between the House and the Chicken Yard

Despite her health problems, Flannery's creativity flourished at Andalusia. There she completed *Wise Blood,* published in 1952, and went on to write *A Good Man Is Hard to Find,* a collection of short stories published in 1955. Her second novel, *The Violent Bear It Away,* followed in 1960. *Everything That Rises Must Converge*, her second collection of stories, appeared posthumously in 1965. Four years later, *Mystery and Manners,* a collection of Flannery's essays edited by Sally and Robert Fitzgerald, made its debut, followed in 1971 by *The Complete Stories.* There was more to come: in 1979, Sally Fitzgerald published *The Habit of Being,* an astonishing array of over 700 of Flannery's letters. She had begun writing these in 1948 and continued writing them until shortly before her death in 1964.

Although many hundreds of Flannery's letters, published and unpublished, are still in existence, she was not prone to saving the ones she received. Thus, there are few remaining examples of the flood of letters that flowed *into* Andalusia. She confessed to a correspondent that she disliked hoarding documents: "About every two months, I become oppressed by paper and I lay about me tearing up every scrap I can get my hands on. If I ever go berserk it will take this form." She described herself as "a maniac killer of public documents."[31]

She certainly didn't feel compelled to keep such letters for posterity, for Flannery believed there would be no biographies written about her. She thought that "lives spent between the house and the chicken yard do not make exciting copy."[32] Indeed, on the surface, her years at Andalusia certainly seem humdrum. She opened her day with prayer, spent a few hours pounding out her fiction on a manual typewriter, and spent the afternoons writing letters and reading. Her letters reveal, however, that there was an extraordinary spiritual life beneath the deceptively ordinary surface. It was anchored in prayer and a solid faith in the teachings of the Catholic Church.

Terrified by Pinocchio

The letters provide engaging snapshots of Flannery's everyday life, and her quirky personality. She tells us, for example, that when she was a child she was terrified by *Alice in Wonderland* and *Pinocchio,* much preferring *Peter Rabbit*.[33] She called her parents by their first names, Ed and Regina. She dreaded birthdays for fear her mother would throw a surprise party for her. As she told a friend, "My idea of hell was the door bursting open and a flock of children pouring in yelling SURPRISE!"[34] She couldn't play chess, but liked the feel of the pieces, and she also enjoyed the peculiar scent of *National Geographic*. After scoring 100 on the written portion of her driving test, she flunked the practical part by losing control of the car.[35] "I barely brought the patrol man back alive," she later reported.[36] And although she did finally get her license, she later went on to knock down a highway sign.[37]

Most of all, the letters reveal a woman who thoroughly enjoyed life. She did not find the rules of her faith onerous, but comforting. She went to Mass faithfully, prayed for her friends, and never tired of reminding visitors to Andalusia that in medieval times the many "eyes" on her peacocks' majestic tails symbolized omniscience, and also represented the "all-seeing" Catholic Church. She also enjoyed poking fun at the local, extremely Irish pastor, as well as pompous Catholic writers whom she tagged the "Cathlick interleckshuls."[38]

"Such a Roman Catholic"

Many readers who revere Flannery's works aren't quite sure what to make of her faith. Literature professors at secular universities eagerly probe her stories yet downplay – or ignore entirely – the signs of her Catholic beliefs. However, as she herself remarked, the tendency to misunderstand her stories was not restricted to non-Catholics. As we shall see, in her day the Catholic press also largely missed the point, because many critics expected her stories to be peopled with nuns and priests rather than Bible-thumping fundamentalist preachers.

The Catholic threads running through her fiction often are subtle. Given that she wrote about country folk living in the Deep South, it made sense for her to people her stories largely with Protestants. However, their themes of the Fall, redemption, and grace are deeply Catholic. "I write the way I do because and only because I am a Catholic," she proclaimed in no uncertain terms.

Further, her faith was integral to more than her writing: she added that if she were not a Catholic, she would have "no reason to write, no reason to see, no reason ever to feel horrified or even to enjoy anything."[39]

Her devotion to her faith irritated some people who weren't hesitant to express distaste for it. In 1972, when she was posthumously honored with the National Book Award, her publisher, Robert Giroux, was preparing himself to receive the award when he was suddenly startled by an author's question: "Do you really think Flannery O'Connor was a great writer? She's such a Roman Catholic." The person making this bigoted remark didn't realize its underlying perceptiveness, for as Ralph C. Wood has so astutely pointed out, her life and her work cannot be understood apart from her faith.[40]

More Than a Hermit Writer

Flannery refused to reduce her stories to one simple meaning because she believed that a good story always had mystery in it, even to its creator, and spoke with different voices to different readers. However, in her letters, Flannery lays her proverbial cards on the table and reveals her deepest religious beliefs. The letters show that she was more than a storyteller, more than a woman suffering from a debilitating illness, and more than a hermit writer on a farm: she was a compassionate, brilliant spiritual director and an eloquent defender of the central truths of Catholicism.

Over the years, Flannery became a model for her friends, especially Atlanta clerk Betty Hester, who sought her advice on the Catholic faith as well as writing, and two college students, Alfred Corn and Roslyn Barnes, who needed encouragement on their faith journeys. As a spiritual director, Flannery explained tough theological concepts and defended the Church against various attacks. She also modeled Christ's love and mercy.

Picking Up Her Cross

When a cousin insisted that she go on a pilgrimage to Lourdes to find healing for lupus, Flannery had no desire to comply. In the end, however, she made the necessary sacrifices and joined the other pilgrims. As her symptoms from lupus worsened, she picked up her crutches – and her cross – with little fanfare, but plenty of humor and humility. And right to the end, she exulted in God's creation, finding joy in the strutting, squawking birds and mischievous burros that made their homes at Andalusia.

But this mysterious mix of writer, bird-lover, humorist, Southerner, Catholic, and critic was not perfect. There were times when she used harsh language that to this day has some people branding her a racist, although the truth definitely lies elsewhere. There were times when she was overly critical of individual clergymen, although she shaped passionate and eloquent defenses when the priesthood came under attack.

A Ministry of Writing

Flannery admitted that writing fiction was hard work for her. Sometimes she'd work on a story for months and then throw all the drafts away. Her letters reveal another side to her, however: a non-fiction writer who used her editorial talents to help others. When the nuns from an Atlanta cancer home asked for help in writing a book, for example, she was highly dubious at first, but she soon overcame her misgivings and gave the project her time and energy. When friends sent her stories to review, she pored over the manuscripts and sent them detailed comments. And although she at times complained bitterly about it, she reviewed books for the local diocesan newspaper.

Who then was Flannery O'Connor? She was a woman who practiced her faith by overcoming obstacles and celebrating what she loved. Despite harsh suffering from her illness, she continued praying, cracking jokes, welcoming visitors, writing stories, and churning out hundreds of letters. She bristled when anyone tried to brand her a saint, but it's easy to see why someone might use that description. She was, all in all, a holy woman who deeply loved Christ. She was a woman who had been given much grace.

I

Her Interior Life

She could never be a saint, but she thought she could be a martyr if they killed her quick.

—*"A Temple of the Holy Ghost"*

CHAPTER 1

The Province of Joy:
Angels, Demons, and Daily Prayers

Flannery was a creature of habit. She set aside a definite amount of time each morning for writing, and she did her best to avoid interruptions. On Sundays, she and her mother headed to Sacred Heart Catholic Church in Milledgeville, where they attended the 7:15 a.m. Mass, sitting in the same pew each week.[1] Her letters reveal another deeply ingrained habit: her commitment to daily prayer. Although her illness curtailed her energy and limited the hours she could give to writing, she still made prayer a top priority. She also advised her friends that prayer could strengthen their faith better than delving into religious tomes and studying theological arguments.[2] In her daily life, she took her cue from communities of monks and nuns that interweave prayer and work throughout the day. Along with the prayers found in her breviary, a simple, leather-bound book, she also said a favorite daily prayer to the Archangel Raphael.

3

Socking the Angel

It is a bit ironic that Flannery said a daily prayer to an angel, since as a child she had developed something she described as "anti-angel aggression." When she was eight and learned from the sisters that each person had a guardian angel, always at one's side, little Mary Flannery was none too thrilled, perhaps because she thought of him as spying on her. "From eight to twelve years, it was my habit to seclude myself in a locked room every so often and with a fierce (and evil) face, whirl around in a circle with my fists knotted, socking the angel."[3] She knew she couldn't hurt him, but she still endeavored to dirty his feathers. "My dislike of him was poisonous," she confessed to her friend Betty Hester in 1956. "I'm sure I even kicked at him and landed on the floor."[4]

By the time she was twelve she had overcome this particular fixation, and with the passing years she gradually forgot that angels existed. When she was about twenty-nine, however, she received a card from *The Catholic Worker* with a prayer to St. Raphael on it: "This led me to find out eventually what angels were, or anyway what they were not. And what they are not is a big comfort to me."[5] Although she did not specify "what they are not," we can infer that this avid reader of St. Thomas Aquinas's *Summa Theologica* eventually discovered that angels are not heavenly spies, trailing us around and "tattling" on us to God, but rather are sent by God to help us grow in grace. Once she had this change of attitude, the same woman who had once tried to flatten one angel found herself regularly beseeching another for protection.

Heaven as Our True Home

St. Raphael, whose name means "God has healed," is one of three archangels mentioned in Scripture. It is very possible that Flannery's particular attraction for this angel was connected to her own hope for healing, although she never divulged this fact in her letters. It is also likely that her prayer card showed a typical depiction of St. Raphael, portrayed standing next to a young man carrying a fish.

According to the Old Testament story in the Book of Tobit, Tobias's father had been struck blind and could no longer work, so he asked his son to make a journey to collect a debt for him. A stranger accompanied Tobias on the journey, and when the young man confronted a huge, dangerous fish, the stranger told him how to defend himself. Later, this same stranger instructed Tobias to use parts of the fish to expel a demon from his bride and to cure his father's blindness. When in Tobit 12:15, the stranger finally revealed his identity, he said, "I am Raphael, one of the seven holy angels who present the prayers of the saints and enter into the presence of the glory of the Lord."

The beautiful prayer to St. Raphael, found in the appendix, depicts life as a journey to heaven, described as our true home. As she prayed, Flannery would have beseeched St. Raphael, the angel of "happy meetings," to guide her toward "those who are waiting for us" in heaven. She would ask that her everyday actions be imbued with the angel's joy, as well as petitioning Raphael to place a special personal request at the feet of "Him on whose unveiled Face" he gazes.[6]

Crushed by Life's Sorrows

It is especially moving to envision Flannery relying on this prayer toward the end of her life, when lupus was taking its grim toll. We can picture her in her small, humble room at Andalusia, praying for the strength to bear whatever the future held. When she felt "crushed by the separations and sorrows of life,"[7] she might have begged the strong archangel to remember the weak. The prayer also emphasizes the Christian belief that our lives in this fallen world are flawed and fleeting. It speaks of heaven as "the province of joy," which exists beyond our troubled world, the "region of thunder."[8]

For a young woman with a serious illness, this daily prayer must have brought comfort, since heaven is depicted as peaceful, serene, and "bright with the resplendent glory of God."[9] The prayer was part of Flannery's life for many years. In 1964, about a month before her death, she shared it with a New York friend in a letter.[10] Flannery also took the well-worn prayer card to the hospital when she was gravely ill, and after her death, it was discovered on her bedside table there.[11]

"My Devil Has a Name"

It would make little sense for someone who believed so strongly in angels to deny the existence of demons, and Flannery never made this mistake. Unfortunately, popular culture often portrays devils as little red imps with pitchforks, but she knew the truth lay elsewhere. Lucifer was very real to Flannery. He certainly was not a comic book figure, nor was he a mere symbol. "My Devil has a name, a history, and a definite plan," she wrote in a letter to writer John Hawkes. "His name is Lucifer, he's a fallen angel, his sin is pride, and his aim is the destruction of the Divine plan." She disagreed with Hawkes's view of the devil, especially his belief that the devil was co-equal to God, rather than God's creature. Hawkes also apparently believed that pride was the devil's virtue, not his sin. Trying to set Hawkes straight, she wrote firmly, "My Devil is objective and yours is subjective."[12]

Flannery expounded further on her beliefs about the devil in her review of *Evidence of Satan in the Modern World*, published in 1962. There she noted that it was ironic that "in these evil times we should need fresh evidence of the existence of Satan." She mentioned Baudelaire's suggestion that the devil's greatest wile was persuading people that he didn't exist. "The Christian drama is meaningless without Satan," she emphasized. It seems that Anglicans at the time were unknowingly proving Baudelaire's point, as they considered deleting references to the devil from their catechism. We can imagine Flannery sighing and rolling her eyes as she wrote, "Such is the trend of the times."[13]

The disturbing trend of denying the reality of the devil reared its ugly head after her novel *The Violent Bear It Away* was published. In the book, shortly after his grandfather's death a character named Tarwater begins hearing the voice of a stranger in his head. The stranger tempts him to abandon his belief in Jesus, while also assuring him the devil does not exist. Replying to Hawkes, who had written her about the book, Flannery corrected him sharply: "I certainly do mean Tarwater's friend to be the Devil."[14] She emphasized in another letter that she wanted to be sure that "the Devil gets identified as the Devil and not simply taken for this or that psychological tendency."[15] Students in a writing class had discussed the identity of the voice and had arrived at some odd conclusions, she told Hawkes. Only one thought it came from the devil. To her dismay, the rest thought it was a "voice of light," which would "liberate Tarwater from that 'horrible old man.'"[16]

In the book, Tarwater is drugged and then raped by a "pale, lean, old-looking young man with deep hollows under his cheekbones," who drives a lavender-and-cream colored car. Flannery told her editor, Robert Giroux, that she had received a rather depressing letter from a reader who didn't comprehend the "significance" of Tarwater's violation by this man. The letter writer didn't understand the religious symbolism, she added, because of his own self-confessed ignorance. "But if the modern reader is so far de-Christianized that he doesn't recognize the Devil when he sees him," she wrote plaintively, "I fear for the reception of the book."[17]

Annoying Devotions and a "Garish-Looking Book"

In Flannery's day, every Mass was followed by a prayer to the Archangel Michael, which re-affirmed the Catholic belief in the reality – and destructiveness – of the devil. In this vividly worded prayer, Catholics invoke St. Michael's help in defending them against the "snares" of Satan and other evil spirits, who prowl throughout the world "seeking the ruin of souls."[18] Given her strong sense of Satan's power, this prayer surely would have suited Flannery as did the one to the Archangel Raphael.

However, there were other popular Catholic devotions that she found annoying, and in her typical, outspoken fashion, she didn't hesitate to express her opinion. She had little use for prayers with highly emotional language, for example, and she was not a big fan of novenas. As she noted in a letter written in 1956, "I think of novenas the same way I think of the hideous Catholic churches you all too frequently find yourself in, that is, after a time I cease to see them even though I'm in them." Although she admitted that the discipline of praying for a nine-day stretch might prove beneficial, she generally disliked prayers by "saints-in-an-emotional state." For her, emotions were private, and she wasn't inclined to dress herself up in someone else's feelings: "I can never describe my heart as 'burning' to the Lord (who knows better) without snickering."[19]

Flannery was well aware that some people judged Catholics harshly for praying and partaking of the sacraments with little outward emotion. In a 1959 letter to university professor T. R. Spivey, a Protestant, she explained that lack of visible emotion should not be taken as a sign that nothing is going on in the person's heart because, "We don't believe that grace is something you have to feel." She acknowledged that Catholics distrusted emotional reactions to the sacraments, but also emphasized that it was unfair to judge Catholics as going about their religion mechanically because "this is something only God knows."[20]

There is a compelling scene in "A Temple of the Holy Ghost" (one of three stories featuring Catholic characters) that illustrates a distinctly Catholic approach to prayer. A little Southern girl is attending Benediction, a worship service that centers on the exposition and adoration of the Communion Host, which Catholics revere as the Body of Christ. Prayers during Benediction are ritualized and formal, but during the service, the child's heart begins to soften. She had entered the chapel with her head crammed with critical thoughts, but now, as she realizes she is in God's presence, the flow of ugly thoughts ceases and she speaks directly to God in her own words: "Hep me not to be so mean."[21]

Overly emotional prayers annoyed Flannery, but the staid, dignified prayers in a book called *A Short Breviary for Religious and the Laity* suited her just fine. She sent a breviary to Hester in 1956, describing it, with its cranberry cover and pink-edged pages, as a "rather garish-looking book." In sending the gift, Flannery didn't want to seem to be imposing an obligation on her friend, so she downplayed the book's significance. "Don't think I am suggesting you read [the prayers] every day. It's just a good thing to know about."[22]

This letter reveals a great deal about Flannery's own prayer habits. Using her "garish-looking book," she would say morning and night prayers, including psalms and other biblical passages. And despite her jokes about the book's appearance, she admitted that the prayers were important to her.[23] So many prayer books, in her estimation, were awful, while prayers based on the liturgy, such as the ones in the breviary, she considered safe.

That these prayers were central to her life is evident in a letter written seven years later. At that time, Flannery confessed to her Catholic schoolteacher correspondent, Janet McKane, that she wasn't good at practicing St. Ignatius's method of meditation and also had trouble keeping her mind from straying when she said the rosary. However, she was still faithfully saying morning and night prayers from the breviary.[24]

"Open, O Lord, My Mouth"

Monks divide their days between *ora* and *labora* – prayer and work – pausing from their labor every few hours to chant psalms and say prayers in their breviaries. Traditionally, they pray Matins after midnight and then rise at dawn to pray Lauds, the morning song of praise. Prime is said between six and nine a.m., and asks a blessing upon one's daily work. The other prayers include Terce, between nine a.m. and noon; Sext, between noon and three p.m; Vespers at sundown; and Compline before going to sleep at night.

Flannery's day began with morning prayers that dedicated her writing to God. We can picture the Abbess of Andalusia each morning picking up her little book and praying silently, "Open, O Lord, my mouth that I may praise Thy holy Name; cleanse my heart from all vain, perverse and distracting thoughts... so that I may pray... attentively and devoutly."[25] Next, she would recite an Our Father and Hail Mary and then ask God to guard her heart and tongue from strife, protect her eyes from evil sights, and close her ears to vanities.[26]

Each morning of her week featured different psalms. Sunday opened with Psalm 119, a reminder of the blessings that come to God's faithful people.[27] On Monday, her day began with the stirring question of Psalm 24: "Who shall go up unto the mountain of the Lord and who shall stand in His holy place?" and the reply: "He who is innocent of hands and pure of heart..."[28] A note by the monks reminded readers that life was a journey towards heaven, something that the prayer to St. Raphael also emphasized.

Each Tuesday morning, Psalm 25 emphasized the need to clasp God's hand with childlike confidence.[29] Wednesday began with the prayer of the innocent in Psalm 26: "Redeem me and be merciful to me!"[30] Every Thursday, Flannery recited lines from the well-known Psalm 23, especially meaningful for people near death: "The Lord is my shepherd and nothing is wanting to me."[31] Longing for heaven was Friday morning's theme, while Saturday's psalm featured a reminder of God's loving kindness.[32] Her morning ritual closed with a Scripture reading in the breviary, as well as the classic Catholic remembrance of the dead: "Eternal rest grant unto them, O Lord. And let perpetual light shine upon them."[33]

The Devil as a Roaring Lion

Flannery admitted that there were times when she neglected her night prayers, perhaps because in bed she sometimes read a theology book instead. However, when she did pick up her breviary at night, she would have needed extra time, since the prayers are rather lengthy. Intended to help us make peace with God before going to sleep, the prayers offer protection against the night's long stretch of darkness, which traditionally symbolizes the devil. Thus the night readings contain a somber warning from 1 Peter 5: 8-9: "Be sober and watch, because your adversary the devil as a roaring lion goeth about seeking whom he may devour."

All in all, night prayers would have given Flannery a vivid reminder of death, but certainly not in a morbid way. Instead, the breviary connects death with the serenity of sleep, as one poetic prayer suggests: "May Almighty God grant us a peaceful night and a perfect end."[34] Compline also has a hymn with lyrics asking for God's defense against evil dreams and "nightly fears and fantasies."[35] Flannery's day would end with the repetition of the beautifully trusting words of Jesus on the Cross: "Into Thy hands, O Lord, I commend my spirit." There also was a lovely request for God to protect her under the shadow of his wings and for the holy angels to watch over her.

A Dark Night of the Soul

There were stretches of time when Flannery grappled with a fear all too familiar to many writers, namely that her wellspring of creativity was drying up. It was at those times she turned to others for spiritual help. Two days before Christmas, 1958, she wrote Father McCown to tell him that she was at a critical point in her novel *The Violent Bear It Away*. "I need your prayers about it," she said. "I would rather finish this novel right than be able to walk at all. It requires a lot more than I have."[36]

On March 4, 1962, she reminded him that she had been writing for sixteen years and was concerned about a lack of inspiration. She plaintively asked him to pray that "the Lord will send me some more." Experiencing something like a writer's Dark Night of the Soul, she feared that she had "exhausted [her] original potentiality" and she expressed a poignant longing for the "kind of grace that deepens perception, a new shot of life or something."[37]

Three months later, she expressed a similar concern about her writing to Sister Julie, a Dominican nun at Our Lady of Perpetual Help Home in Atlanta. Although she was writing every day, Flannery admitted that nothing much was happening: "The brew [has] not begun to thicken yet." She added simply: "Please pray it will."[38] A year later, when Flannery asked another nun for prayers, she said she doubted her ability to continue writing. "I can't do again what I know I can do well, and the larger things that I need to do now, I doubt my capacity for doing."[39]

The Light of Day

Flannery's health was rapidly deteriorating when she wrote the above letters, but her requests for prayers centered more on her stories than her health. All along, the focus of Flannery's life was her writing, not her ailments, which she tended to bear with humor and equanimity. Physical discomforts she could shrug off, but not hours staring at a blank page in the typewriter. Thus, as she struggled with writer's block, a serious creative malady, it made sense that she would ask for her friends' prayers. And it wasn't long before the dark night was over and the words began flowing again. *The Violent Bear It Away,* the book for which she had asked Father McCown's prayers, was published in 1960, about two years after she had written to him.

And despite Flannery's increasing health problems and diminished energy, new stories continued to emerge from the hermitage at Andalusia. In July of 1962, about four months after writing to Father McCown expressing her longing for a "new shot of life," Flannery wrote another friend to report that the writing was going quite well.[40] Another four months passed, and on November 5, 1962 she told her editor, Robert Giroux, that she had seven stories written, and she might call her next collection *Everything That Rises Must Converge*.[41] She didn't realize it, of course, but that name would stick, although the collection would not be published until after her death.

Shut-Mouth Spirituality

Many people have difficulties praying, but they may be hesitant to admit it. Flannery, however, was forthcoming in confessing her trials. In 1964, she assured her New York pen pal, Janet McKane, that she prayed for her, but it was in her own fashion, "which is not a very good one." Calling herself a not very good "pray*er*," she said her type of spirituality was "almost completely shut-mouth." She went on to say that piously written books did nothing to help matters. In fact, she believed "They corrupt most people's ears if nothing else." She did praise a book by C.S. Lewis on prayer, although she admitted that it hadn't helped her pray any better.[42]

Nonetheless, she was faithful to prayer. When McKane fell ill and had to be hospitalized, Flannery immediately picked up her rosary beads, and even managed to stay awake throughout five decades, which was unusual. "I wish I could send you something or do something for you," she wrote her friend plaintively, "but that will have to wait." Since she herself was hospitalized at the time, prayers were the only gift she could offer, but she knew they were important, that "the rosary is at least tangible." She ended the letter with her usual "Cheers" and said that she would see how many decades she could pray that night on her friend's behalf.[43]

For the Repose of My Soul

Catholic Masses – the Church's principal and most powerful prayer – are offered each day for the special intentions of the living, and for the repose of the souls of the dead. Well aware of the importance of prayers and the Mass, Flannery wanted to be sure these would continue on her behalf after her death. Thus, in her last will and testament, signed on April 18, 1958, she wrote: "It is my wish and desire... that my executrix... set aside the sum of $100.00 for the purpose to have masses said for the repose of my soul."[44]

Of course, Flannery knew that Masses could be celebrated in her memory without a monetary donation. Still, she set aside this generous amount, perhaps as a reminder to Regina to schedule the Masses at Sacred Heart Church. The practice of leaving directions and money in one's will for the repose of one's soul was fairly standard practice for Catholics in Flannery's day. It is a wonderful reminder that the soul is more important than the material possessions accumulated in life.

✠ ✠ ✠ ✠

For those who wonder how Flannery faced death with such apparent courage and grace, the answer doesn't lie in psychoanalyzing her or examining her childhood.

Rather, the source of her ability to endure largely lies in her sacramental and prayer life. Despite her admission that she was not very skilled at petitioning God, Flannery's letters reveal that her life was anchored solidly in prayer. By the time she sat down at her typewriter and plunked out the first word, she had already devoted the entire day's work to God through the reading of her morning psalms.

As we have seen, her devotional habits were characteristically Catholic. She relied on formal prayer books more than spontaneous prayers and appreciated devotions that were linked to the liturgy. Prayers recited aloud at Mass or read silently from books are unchanging, just as God is, offering a sense of the Absolute and a firm spiritual anchor in a shifting world. Flannery knew she could rely upon them even on days when she was worried about her writing or weakened from illness – just as she knew she could rely on the intercessory prayers of Mary, the saints, and the Archangel Raphael.

As we have seen, the prayers she turned to each day painted a picture of death in spiritual terms. For those who believe in the promises of Christ, death is the doorway to a new realm, a place where every tear will be wiped away. And even if Flannery was largely a loner, spending her days at the typewriter and forging friendships through the distance of letters, she drew great strength from her spiritual companions in heaven.

CHAPTER 2

The Little Way at Andalusia: Devotion to the Saints

*A*s any Catholic can attest, saints play a big role in our faith journeys. They are seen as spiritual models, friends, and intercessors, as well as members of our mystical family. "Saints are little Christs," writes Peter Kreeft, who describes them as windows showing us the divine light.[1] Flannery would have agreed with Kreeft's description when it came to certain favorite saints whom she especially cherished. However, she was wary of excessive devotions to saints that were in danger of giving rise to what she called "pious pap."[2]

Everything but the Snakes

We have seen how Flannery was far from sentimental, cringing at prayers that were obviously intended to elicit a particular emotion. It is little wonder, then, that despite her Irish ancestry, she found St. Patrick's Day celebrations grossly exaggerated, and showed her disdain for "the great feast" by commemorating Grover Cleveland's birthday the following day.[3] She was especially outraged when the local pastor, whom she sarcastically referred to as "his reverence," placed a statue of St. Patrick "up smack in the front" of Sacred Heart church. She complained bitterly to her Jesuit friend Father McCown: "He has everything about him but the snakes – a purple shirt, a green robe, an orange book, white gloves, gold hat – and is holding up as if for sale or edification... a shamrock."[4]

The Little Way

Fortunately, one saint whom Flannery admired had not been adopted by any ethnic group: Thérèse of the Child Jesus, often called the Little Flower. Born Marie Francoise Thérèse Martin in Alencon, a small town in northern France in 1873, Thérèse entered the convent in Lisieux when she was just fifteen, and she died from tuberculosis nine years later. Her life might sound quite unremarkable, but her autobiography, *Story of a Soul*, reveals an extraordinary, resilient spirit. It was, in fact, the little saint's iron will and heroism that endeared her to Flannery.

In *Story of a Soul*, Thérèse wrote about a revolutionary path to Christ, which she called "the little way." As a sickly nun living behind convent walls, Thérèse realized that she was incapable of grandiose accomplishments, so she decided to walk a simpler path, one based on Matthew 18:1-3 where Jesus tells his disciples, "Truly I say to you, unless you turn and become like little children, you will never enter the kingdom of heaven." For St. Thérèse, the way of spiritual childhood meant making moment-to-moment sacrifices out of love for Christ.

Despite the deceptively simple title, her little way involved huge effort, because it required surrendering herself to Christ and placing her trust in him completely. It also demanded great sacrifices. One example of a down-to-earth sacrifice that Thérèse made, over and over, involved another nun in the convent whose personality clashed sharply with her own. Thérèse found everything about this nun disagreeable, but she swallowed her dislike and faithfully followed the "little way" by treating this woman with love. Remarkably, Thérèse's ability to hide her natural antipathy worked so well that the woman came to believe she was Thérèse's favorite.[5]

Funny Little Noises

The little French nun, hidden in her cloister, and the outspoken Southern writer, hunkered down in her humble room at Andalusia, shared many things in common. Flannery's descriptions of the backwoods characters in her stories often had readers wiping tears of laughter from their eyes, and it seems that St. Thérèse had a similar talent for making people laugh. According to Bernard Bro, she was known for entertaining the nuns behind the cloister walls by doing impersonations that captured, in hilarious detail, the voices and mannerisms of other people.[6]

As a writer, Thérèse shared Flannery's ability to describe events vividly and to convey the small details that bring people to life on a page. There was, for example, one nun who unknowingly broke the silence during meditation in the chapel, driving poor Thérèse nearly to distraction: "As soon as this nun came in, she used to begin making a funny little noise which sounded like two shells being rubbed together."[7] Instead of laughing, shouting, or screaming, however, Thérèse kept still, and she did something that was truly amazing: "I concentrated on listening to it as if it were a magnificent concert, and my entire meditation was spent in offering this concert to Jesus."[8]

Doing Away with the Icing

St. Thérèse was a model for Flannery in many ways. The little nun suffered terribly from tuberculosis and died quite young, while Flannery battled a serious illness for many years before her own early death, an illness that prevented her from fasting and visiting the sick. "I can't even kneel down to say my prayers," she admitted at one point. However, as Paul Elie wisely noted, Flannery resigned herself to her physical condition, and she transformed her suffering by modeling herself after Thérèse and her little way: "[Flannery] believed that 'every opportunity for performing any kind of charity is something to be snatched at.'"[9] Flannery's version of the little way meant making sacrifices, large and small, from the confines of her room at Andalusia, where she worked tirelessly on her stories and churned out hundreds of letters over the years. Sometimes a single letter from Flannery, crafted with great love and concern, could bring relief to a suffering friend.

Even if she had much in common with Thérèse, Flannery bristled at being called a mystic or a saint herself, protesting, "I do not lead a holy life."[10] And in her no-nonsense way, she also abhorred stories about saints that made them seem sickeningly sweet and impossibly holy. Many of these, unfortunately, were about poor St. Thérèse, who has often been depicted surrounded by roses and wearing a very pious expression.

No wonder Flannery was delighted with a 1955 book called *Two Portraits of St. Teresa of Lisieux,* written by Father Etienne Robo, who tried to show the real person beneath the often saccharine surface. When she reviewed the book, Flannery praised him for doing away with "the roses, little flowers, and the other icing." Father Robo claimed that photos of Thérèse had been touched up, after her death, by the Carmelite nuns, who wanted to accentuate her beauty. Flannery said that the originals showed the nun as round-faced, determined, and comical looking,[11] while the tailored versions rendered her face "sweetly characterless."[12] Flannery, clearly pleased that Robo approached Thérèse's life with humor and honesty, paid him a big compliment by adding, "The book has greatly increased my devotion to her."[13]

When Flannery's review of *Two Portraits* appeared in the diocesan newspaper, *The Bulletin,* in May of 1956, she told readers, "Those of us who have been repulsed by popular portraits of the life of St. Thérèse of Lisieux and at the same time attracted by her iron will and heroism... will be cheered to learn... that this reaction is not entirely perverse." She added that the author showed how in other biographies the saint's life had been subject to artifice, "to make it more edifying," and she applauded him for uncovering the real saint in her "very human and terrible greatness."[14]

This "human and terrible greatness" is not something often associated with the saint called the "Little Flower." However, in Flannery's way of thinking, all human beings struggled with the ordinary trials and tribulations of life, and to suggest that saints were an exception made them unapproachable. In a letter written in 1963, she emphasized that an ideal and completely unsullied form of Christianity didn't exist because "anything the human being touches, even Christian truth, he deforms slightly in his own image." She added: "Even the saints do this. I take it to be the effects of Original Sin."[15]

It seems likely that St. Thérèse herself would have applauded the goal of portraying saints without the fake "icing." Evidently, Thérèse had once expressed dismay about the way some preachers had heavily embroidered the Blessed Virgin Mary's life. True, according to Catholic teaching the Blessed Virgin was not touched by sin, but she still was a human being, a mother, and a wife, and Thérèse complained that some preachers made her "so different from us ordinary human beings that... they raise her as much beyond our love as beyond our imitation."[16]

The Church as Gospel Reader

Flannery was well aware of common Protestant criticisms of Catholic devotion to Mary, the Mother of God. Some typical accusations apparently once came in a letter from her friend Betty Hester, motivating Flannery to elucidate a cogent defense of the Church's position. Writing on January 13, 1956, she pointed out that although Protestants often condemn devotions to Mary as "unscriptural," in fact such practices are based on Scripture, and anyone acquainted with Catholic liturgy would be aware that "the Church... is no less a Gospel reader than the separated brethren."[17]

Many Catholics regularly ask for Mary's intercession, leading some Protestants to question why they don't "go directly to God." Writing to Hester, Flannery provided the scriptural reason for this practice by pointing out that Christ performed his first miracle at Mary's request. She also reminded Hester that, as Christ was dying on the Cross, he gave his mother to John (the "Beloved Disciple") and John to her,[18] and in that moment Mary became mother to all Christians as well.

Starving for Sleep

Although Flannery strove to adhere to all the Catholic Church's teachings on faith and morals, there were some optional devotions and practices that left her cold, and she did not hesitate to voice her opinion about them. She described herself to a friend as a "long-standing avoider of May processions and such-like nun-inspired doings," confessing that she was quite thankful "the Church doesn't teach those things are necessary."[19]

Even though she was no fan of processions, Flannery was devoted to Mary. Once, after struggling with long bouts of insomnia due to heavy doses of cortisone she was taking for her illness – "I once did without [sleep] almost all the time for several weeks," she wrote in a letter in 1955, adding that she had been "starving to go to sleep" – she began thinking of sleep as metaphorically connected with the Mother of God. Waxing unusually tender, Flannery observed, "Life without her would be equivalent to me to life without sleep, and as she contained Christ for a time, she seems to contain our life in sleep for a time, so that we are able to wake up in peace."[20]

The Red-Hot Poker

Thomas Aquinas was another saint who gained Flannery's deep respect and affection. "I feel I can personally guarantee that St. Thomas loved God," she affirmed in 1955, "because for the life of me I cannot help loving St. Thomas." Her admiration for this Dominican friar and theologian, born in 1225, was so great that she often read a few pages of his quite difficult work, the *Summa Theologica*, before going to sleep. She joked that sometimes her mother would come in and tell her to turn off the light, and she would then reply, in pseudo-Thomistic style, "On the contrary, I answer that the light, being eternal and limitless, cannot be turned off. Shut your eyes."[21]

Flannery would have been quite familiar with the story of this saint's life, especially one oft-told account of how his temper was roused in defense of his purity. As a young man at the University of Naples, Thomas had encountered some Dominican friars whom he grew to greatly admire. When he told his family that he wanted to join their order, they were incensed that the noble-born Thomas would want to be a mendicant. Apparently his brothers hatched a plan to divert him from the religious life by sending a prostitute to his room to seduce him.

In Flannery's opinion, the mystically oriented St. John of the Cross might have reacted by saying to the woman, "Daughter, let us consider this."[22] But St. Thomas, ordinarily a gentle and slow-moving man, grabbed a red-hot poker from the fireplace and drove the terrified woman out of the room. Thomas outlasted his family's objections, and joined the Dominican order in 1244.

It's little wonder that Flannery admired St. Thomas so much. The drama of the red-hot poker scene would fit nicely in one of her stories, where characters often receive spiritual insights in swift and shocking ways. The prostitute in question might have been as startled as Mrs. Turpin, a self-satisfied Christian lady in "Revelation" who has her comeuppance in a doctor's waiting room. Instead of wielding a poker, a girl named Mary Grace hurls a book across the room, hitting Mrs. Turpin squarely on the head and calling her a "wart hog from hell." As horrifying as the moment is, it leads Mrs. Turpin later to re-evaluate her prejudices against poor people and black servants.

As a writer, Flannery also appreciated St. Thomas for defining the necessary ingredients of art, which he said were goodness, truth, and beauty. In a letter written in 1956, she expressed her dislike for a particular novel (*Affair of the Heart*) that clashed with this definition and seemed mere propaganda rather than true literature: "The novel is an art form and when you use it for anything other than art, you pervert it." This idea, she said, was not her invention. "I got it from St. Thomas (via Maritain) who allows that art is wholly concerned with the good of that which is made."[23] Her point was that a novel should not have a utilitarian end. It should not be a mouthpiece for an author eager to promote a social or religious agenda. Perhaps she had in mind certain Catholic reviewers who had harshly criticized her books because they'd wanted her to champion her faith by promoting explicitly Catholic messages and populating her stories with Catholic characters.

Shocking Moments of Grace

As an author who showed the effects of grace in her fiction, Flannery would have been well aware of Thomas Aquinas's insights on this topic. St. Thomas delineated two kinds of grace: there is the habitual kind, quietly coming from reception of the sacraments and giving us spiritual strength, and another, more dramatic, form that involves God's intervention in human actions.[24] In her fictional worlds, Flannery often portrays the vivid effects of Aquinas's second kind of grace. Divine intervention occurs in a shocking way to illuminate dramatically how one of her characters either accepts or rejects this divine gift.

In "Revelation," a character has to be clobbered on the head before having a change of heart. Grace comes in an even more dramatic way in "A Good Man Is Hard to

Find" when an entire family is massacred by an escaped convict who calls himself "The Misfit." Moments before he kills her, the grandmother has a strange awakening, feeling sudden sympathy for The Misfit. Flannery wrote to John Hawkes on December 26, 1959, explaining that when the grandmother realizes that The Misfit, in a mysterious sense, is connected to her, this is the moment of spiritual insight.[25] She realizes that he is, in a sense, one of her own children, just as everyone is a child of God. Feeling a strong rush of compassion, the old woman reaches out to express affection for the man, but The Misfit is horrified by the gesture and shoots her.

Writing to another author in 1960, Flannery said, "It's the moment of grace for her anyway – a silly old woman – but it leads him to shoot her. This moment of grace excites the devil to frenzy."[26] On the mundane level, The Misfit's action is an unspeakable act of violence, and the scene may explain why many people cringe when reading Flannery's stories. However, as an author who fully embraced the reality of heaven and hell, Flannery believed that the old woman's life didn't end with her bodily destruction. And in a very odd twist of events, The Misfit is instrumental in the grandmother's conversion of heart and acceptance of divine grace. Until the moment she reaches out to touch him, she has been depicted as terribly selfish and largely responsible for the series of mishaps leading to the final tragedy that befalls the family.

Flannery talked about the importance of death when she addressed a college audience in 1963. She described the grandmother, who is facing death, as being in "the most significant position life offers the Christian."[27] She added, "Violence is strangely capable of returning my characters to reality and preparing them to accept their moment of grace."[28] In Flannery's Catholic worldview, the grandmother had been delivered of her sin of selfishness right before dying. It was a moment of vivid grace.

Although none of the killings are explicitly described, this story contains some of the most shocking moments in Flannery's repertoire. We read with growing horror as the mother and the children and the father are taken into the woods and massacred just a few yards away from the grandmother. We know in our hearts what comes next, and we wish we could save the old woman. But Flannery shows us that the divine gift of grace often occurs at just such terrifying moments. We might like to think that God's intervention in our lives is accompanied by a nice burst of light and the background music of angels. But Christ came into a bloody and brutal world, and died a horrifying death, and that death changed everything. For Flannery, the fact of the Incarnation, God becoming one of us and dying for us, was the basic lynchpin of the entire universe. God's death on the Cross was the most shocking event imaginable, and yet that event brought salvation to the world. Through untold agony and undying love, grace flowed from the Cross. And in Flannery's stories, God's grace often is offered in the most startling and upsetting situations.

As she herself so lucidly explained it in an essay called "Catholic Novelists," the universe of the Catholic fiction writer is founded on three basic truths of the Faith: the Fall, the Redemption, and the Judgment. However, the secular world doesn't believe these truths, and neither does it believe in sin or the value of suffering. The Catholic writer's dilemma, then, is that "he often finds himself writing in and for a world that is unprepared and unwilling to see the meaning of life as he sees it." This is why, from Flannery's perspective, she resorted to "violent

literary means" as a way to get her Catholic vision across
to a "hostile audience."[29]

✠   ✠   ✠   ✠

The young Virgin Mary's simple response in Luke
1:38 – "Let it be done to me according to your word" –
stands as a model for accepting whatever God plans for
us. In Flannery's life, God's will included her commitment to writing, as well as her suffering from the physical deterioration associated with lupus. It was also his
will that she would remain single and childless, living
with her mother and becoming more dependent on her
day by day.

As we have seen, St. Thérèse's life shows that even
the broken down and the bedridden can serve God in
their own humble ways. Devotion to this saint enabled
Flannery to transform daily suffering into acts of love for
God. And just as Thérèse earned Flannery's admiration
for her strength of character, her endurance in suffering, and her "terrible and human greatness," St. Thomas
became a favorite of Flannery's for his ability to explain,
logically and coherently, the concepts of Christian belief.
His *Summa Theologica* demonstrates that there can be
no contradiction between the truths of faith, based on
divine revelation, and the truths of human reason. As
we will see in the next two chapters, Flannery herself
made use of logic and reason in elucidating the truths of
Catholicism for friends seeking her guidance.

II

Spiritual Director by Mail

They joked a lot where he lived. If he had thought about it before, he would have thought Jesus Christ was a word like "oh" or "damn" or "God," or maybe somebody who had cheated them out of something sometime. When he had asked Mrs. Connin who the man in the sheet in the picture over her bed was, she had looked at him a while with her mouth open. Then she had said, "That's Jesus," and she had kept on looking at him.

—"The River"

CHAPTER 3

Adopted Kin: The Tragic Journey of Betty Hester

A simple impulse can change our lives. This was certainly true for Hazel Elizabeth ("Betty") Hester, a file clerk in Atlanta, who followed an impulse to write a letter to Flannery about her fiction. At a time when many critics misunderstood her stories, Flannery appreciated Hester's insights into them. On July 20, 1955, she wrote back: "Perhaps it is even more startling to me to find someone who recognizes my work for what I try to make it than it is for you to find a God-conscious writer near at hand."[1] Flannery told Hester that her Catholic faith was integral to her writing – and to her whole life. This interchange, arising from Hester's impulse, gave birth to a correspondence and friendship that lasted nine years.

The two women shared much in common. Both were single and living with relatives. Both were avid readers. Hester had aspirations to become a writer, and over the years she would share her own stories with Flannery. Hester was not Catholic, but it wasn't long before questions about religion arose in the weekly interchange of letters, and Flannery began serving as an impromptu spiritual director for her new friend.

The letters written to Hester about the Catholic faith give us crucial glimpses into Flannery's spirituality. We learn from her passionate defense of the Eucharist, for example, that this sacrament was the center of Flannery's life. In fact, it was the grace flowing from this encounter with Christ, along with prayer, that gave her the strength to endure the disease that debilitated and finally killed her. We also see why Flannery was such a powerful spiritual guide for Hester. It was never in her nature to be preachy or holier-than-thou, and there's no evidence of such an attitude in her responses to Hester's questions. She never presented Catholicism as a balm that would heal all her friend's ills; instead, she reminded Hester that at the heart of Christianity there is the Cross. By her heartfelt honesty, and her frank admission of her own shortcomings, Flannery avoided presenting the Faith as welcoming only the perfect and sinless. And when her friend admitted to struggling with terrible guilt over a past sin, Flannery reminded her that Christ offers mercy and forgiveness.

Evangelizing as God's Work

At the beginning of her correspondence with Flannery, Hester found herself attracted to the Catholic faith, but she was resisting its pull. No wonder Flannery's early responses to her new friend give the impression of walking on a tightrope. Flannery was eager to encourage Hester and send her books on Catholicism, but she feared that they might seem "too Catholic." She certainly didn't want to seem pushy, as she admitted in a letter dated January 30, 1956: "I did not want you to think that I was trying to stuff the Church down your throat." And although she dearly wanted to see her friend accept the Faith, Flannery believed that the work of evangelizing was ultimately God's to do: "The Church can't be put forward by anybody but God and one is apt to do great damage by trying."[2] It was only when Hester began asking questions and seeking religious books on her own that Flannery felt comfortable responding.

Hester had a confused picture of Catholicism. She apparently had confessed to Flannery that at times she felt she was being "seduced" by the Church, but she feared that Catholicism would limit her intellectual horizons and require her to shut down her reason. Flannery tried to allay this fear by suggesting just the opposite: "I doubt if your interests get less intellectual as you become more deeply involved in the Church, but... the intellect will take its place in a larger context and will cease to be tyrannical, if it has been." In her opinion, a "tyrannical intellect" was a danger; instead the mind serves best "when it's anchored in the word of God."[3] As for Hester's efforts to withstand "seduction" by the Church, Flannery remarked that her friend's resistance moved her greatly: "God permits it for some reason though it is the devil's greatest work of hallucination."[4]

As a spiritual director, Flannery acted kindly and patiently, assuring her friend that no simple, straightforward path to Catholicism existed. She also told her that a person did not have to be perfect to be received into the Church. In fact, "Most people come to the Church by means the Church does not allow, else there would be no need their getting to her at all." The Church was there to welcome sinners, "which creates much misunderstanding among the smug."[5]

Lunatic or Devil

Hester struggled with belief in the central mystery of Christianity, which is the doctrine of the Incarnation. She apparently respected Christ as an enlightened and virtuous man, but not as God in the flesh. Yet she was corresponding in friendship with a fiercely Catholic woman who embraced the Incarnation as "the ultimate reality."[6] And this woman definitely wanted Hester to understand the inherent contradiction in trying to admire Christ as a wise and moral, but entirely human, person.

In *Mere Christianity*, first published in 1943, C.S. Lewis had described Christ as someone who made outrageous claims, claims that only God could make: that he could forgive sins, that he would judge the world at the end of time. Thus, said Lewis, if Christ were not God, as he claimed, it made no sense to call him a good teacher. Instead, he would best be described as a lunatic or a devil.[7] Flannery echoed Lewis's reasoning in a letter to Hester in August of 1955: "If He was not God, He was no realist, only a liar, and the crucifixion an act of justice."[8]

Despite Flannery's explanation, Hester continued to struggle with the idea of Christ's divinity. For one, this belief seemed to clash with fundamental physical laws, since from a purely scientific standpoint, the virgin birth, the Incarnation, and the Resurrection would be impossible. Writing to Hester on September 6, 1955, Flannery offered a different take on the matter, suggesting that human beings have a limited understanding of physical laws. We understand these laws "as we see them, not as God sees them." In truth, she said, at the heart of human life there are spiritual realities. Revealing her mystical lens on the world, she called the virgin birth, the Incarnation, and the resurrection "the true laws of the flesh and the physical." Death, decay, and destruction she defined as "the suspension of these laws."[9]

A Sinless Body with Sinful Members

There were other stumbling blocks on Hester's road to conversion. One particularly heated concern emerged in the letters after Flannery had shared with Hester the story about St. Thomas Aquinas encountering the prostitute. Commenting on his use of the red-hot poker to scare the woman away, Flannery had commented, "It would be fashionable today to be in sympathy with the woman, but I am in sympathy with St. Thomas."[10]

This remark riled Hester, and in short order Flannery was defending herself – and Aquinas – against charges of fascism. "Find another word than fascist, for me and St. Thomas too," Flannery demanded. She upheld the saint's reaction, saying he knew himself well enough to realize that in such a situation extreme measures were needed. In short, he had to discourage the woman "or she would [have] overcome him." His use of the poker was far from a descent into fascism; she called it being "tolerantly realistic."[11]

Besides, Flannery continued, even if St. Thomas, one member of the Church, had done wrong in brandishing a hot poker to drive out that prostitute, this wasn't enough to accuse the entire Catholic Church of wrong-doing. Flannery emphasized to Hester that "principle must be separated from policy." She explained that she herself on principle disliked force, but might find herself using it, "in which case I would have to convict myself of sin."[12] This distinction between the Church as Christ's mystical body and the actions of individual members was crucial, and it would come up again in the letters.

Emotions and Faith

Many people think faith should be emotionally satisfying. If they go to church and don't feel uplifted, they assume the liturgy failed, and if they don't sense God's presence during a crisis, they conclude that he no longer exists. It seems this was another of Hester's problems, since she apparently had confessed to Flannery that believing in the Incarnation failed to satisfy her emotionally. In reply, Flannery warned that it was dangerous to use feelings as the barometer for deeper truth. She added, "The thought of everyone lolling about in an emotionally satisfying faith is repugnant to me."[13]

She also warned Hester that a faith journey actually might be impeded by emotion because feelings are constantly changing, while the truth is constant. As example, Flannery pointed to the growing atheism of the times, noting that the whole world seemed to be going through a dark night of the soul: "The very notion of God's existence is not emotionally satisfactory anymore for great numbers of people, which does not mean that God ceases to exist."[14]

Dark Nights of the Soul

The emotion topic had to be especially meaningful to Hester, who suffered from depression and who may have hoped that embracing the Catholic faith would help cure her emotional ills. However, Flannery emphasized that even the saints experienced dark nights of the soul in which their faith was far from emotionally satisfying. Worse, their faith might have seemed "hideous, emotionally disturbing, downright repulsive."[15]

At the time Flannery was writing, she was, of course, unaware of Mother Teresa's Dark Night of the Soul. She didn't know that letters would one day reveal how one of the holiest women of the twentieth century had for many years experienced an agonizing sense of God's absence.[16] Mother Teresa continued with her ministry despite the doubts, exemplifying Flannery's point that faith is revealed in actions, rather than feelings.

"The Rest of Life Is Expendable"

Another miracle awaited Hester's embrace as she explored the Catholic faith: the Real Presence of Christ in the Eucharist. After the Reformation, belief in this doctrine died out among most Protestants, who came to regard the bread and wine of Holy Communion as mere symbols. And yet to Flannery, this change of belief made no sense, because Christ would not have altered his teaching. As she pointed out to another correspondent, an impossible shift, an unthinkable contradiction, had occurred after the Reformation: "For fifteen centuries [Christ] taught that the Eucharist was his actual body and blood and thereafter he taught part of his people that it was only a symbol."[17] Shortly before Christmas in 1955, Flannery wrote to Hester, emphasizing her belief that "the Host is actually the body and blood of Christ, not a symbol." She then recounted an experience that beautifully illuminated the depth of her convictions.

About five years earlier, she had attended a dinner hosted by the ex-Catholic writer Mary McCarthy, who according to Flannery "departed the Church at the age of fifteen and is a Big Intellectual."[18] At some point, the hostess felt moved to share with the group her thoughts on the Eucharist. She declared that, when she had received the Host as a child, she had considered it "the Holy Ghost," but she had thereafter come to think of the Eucharist as a symbol – and "a pretty good one."[19]

Flannery had been sitting quietly, but finally she could no longer hold her tongue. "I then said, in a very shaky voice, 'Well, if it's a symbol, to hell with it.'"

We can well imagine how awkward the rest of the dinner conversation must have been! However, it did prompt Flannery later to articulate her deep devotion to the Eucharist. "That was all the defense I was capable of," she told Hester, "but I realize now that this is all I will ever be able to say about it, outside of a story, except that it is the center of existence for me; all the rest of life is expendable."[20]

"Highly Pleased to Be Asked"

About a year after they began exchanging letters, Hester decided that she wanted to be baptized and received into the Catholic Church. This decision delighted Flannery, who wrote on March 24, 1956 to express her joy. Mentioning that she wanted to do something celebratory for her friend, she painted a humorous verbal picture of herself "holding some kind of figurative candle and croaking the proper responses." On a more serious note, she promised to go to Communion for Hester's intentions on Easter morning at Sacred Heart Church. She also remarked that a new bond would develop between them, because Hester would be receiving Holy Communion for the first time, and thus they would be sharing the same "actual food" of the Eucharist. Now they could help each other spiritually: "Your being where you are increases me and the other way around."[21] Hester was baptized in Atlanta a week later, taking Magdalen, in honor of St. Mary Magdalene, for her baptismal name.[22]

A few months later, Hester asked her friend to sponsor her at Confirmation. Flannery wrote back on

May 5 to say she would be "real pleased," and added jovially, "That is, if I read that right and am not just inviting myself." She also asked about her responsibilities, since she had never been a sponsor before. "What's it mean? I am supposed to come and ask you what the fruits of the Holy Ghost are once a year or something?"[23] This had to be a wonderful moment for Flannery, because, although she did not mention this point, surely she realized their spiritual relationship would echo the bond between godparent and godchild at Baptism. It would be eternal.

Horrible History

The letters don't reveal why Hester chose Magdalen as her baptismal name, but Mary Magdalene is mentioned in Scripture as the woman from whom Christ cast out seven devils. Traditionally, she also has been identified with the unnamed sinful woman in Luke 7:36-50, who washes Christ's feet with her tears. The woman's great outpouring of love for Jesus prompts him to forgive the woman's past sins. As we shall see, Hester was deeply troubled about sins in her own past. Evidently, Flannery had some inkling of these, since in her May 5 letter she made reference to her friend's "horrible history."[24]

The letter that reveals the secret in Hester's past was not published in *The Habit of Being*, but it can be found among the collection of original letters from Flannery to Hester, stored in the archives at Emory University. And although the actual word never appears, it's clear from these letters that Hester's secret involved a history of lesbianism,[25] which had led to her dishonorable discharge from the Air Force.[26]

Poor Hester strongly feared her friend's disapproval. In fact, she was so apprehensive that she evidently suggested that she stop writing to Flannery and stop visiting Andalusia. Replying on October 31, 1956, her spiritual director quickly put an end to that notion: "I can't write you fast enough and tell you that it doesn't make the slightest bit of difference in my opinion of you, which is the same as it was, and that is: based solidly on complete respect." Flannery assured her friend that she would share her suffering: "It only hurts me because it has hurt you."[27]

Meaning of the Redemption

The rest of Flannery's response was equally compassionate. "You wonder if it makes any difference to me if you drop out of my existence," she continued in that same letter. She said it would be impossible for her to let that happen. Hester had done her "nothing but good" and, most importantly, the two had forged a lasting spiritual relationship: "I am your sponsor, self-appointed from the time you first wrote to me and appointed by you afterwards, which means that I have a right to stay where I have been put."

This letter shows what an insightful spiritual director Flannery truly was. She didn't merely explain bits of theology to her friend, nor did she simply answer questions. Instead, she did what every Christian is called to do for those who are suffering: she modeled Christ's mercy and love. She herself was no stranger to suffering, yet she downplayed her own struggles: "Compared to what you have experienced in the way of radical misery, I have never had anything to bear in my life but minor irritations."

Indeed, she noted, sometimes a friend's suffering causes more distress than one's own pain: "Job's comforters

were worse off than he was though they didn't know it."
She assured Hester that if knowing about her past would
lighten her burden, "I am doubly glad I know it." She also
gently corrected Hester, who in one of her letters had
apparently referred to herself as a "history of horror."
Flannery responded firmly, "You are not your history," and
reminded Hester of the deepest meaning of the Redemption, which is that we can be freed from our past.

Accepting Forgiveness

In studying Catholic moral teachings, Hester had no
doubt learned that homosexual actions were considered
sinful. She also would have known that she could confess
her sins and receive forgiveness through the Sacrament
of Confession. Yet she was tortured by memories, and her
suffering prompted Flannery to offer still more comfort:
"I have no doubt that you were, as you say, unbearably
guilty, and that you accepted the guilt and found a way to
suffer for it, and that this was for God." Absolution would
have come through the Sacrament, she assured her, but
the hard part came next. "What you have to accept now
is the forgiveness."

Open-minded about Sexuality?

When the contents of this particular letter were
revealed to the public for the first time, a typical secular confusion about Catholic moral teachings ensued.
An article about the letter appeared in the *Atlanta
Journal-Constitution* on May 10, 2007, with a photo of
Flannery prominently displayed above a caption describing her as "open-minded about sexuality, considering her
strong Catholic faith."[28] In fact, though, Flannery was in
no way veering from traditional Catholic teaching. She

was certainly not condoning Hester's past actions, but was instead showing her friend compassion – something completely in keeping with the Church's teaching that homosexuals be accepted with "respect, compassion, and sensitivity."[29]

There is a powerful scene in John 8:1-11 that helps elucidate Flannery's attitude toward her friend. An unnamed woman has been caught in the act of adultery, and is about to be stoned to death by a group of scribes and Pharisees. When they tell Jesus what they plan to do and ask his opinion, he bends down and begins writing on the ground, although we are not told what he wrote. When in John 8:7 he says, "Let him who is without sin among you be the first to throw a stone at her," the men leave, one by one. Left alone with the woman, Jesus doesn't assure her that adultery is simply one acceptable lifestyle choice among many others; instead, he asks her whether anyone has condemned her. Since the men have all left, she answers that no one has. He then tells her that he does not condemn her either, but she should not sin again.

Similarly, Flannery never condemns Hester in the letters, but instead assures her that Hester still has her respect, and that she wants their friendship to continue. But it would be wrong to conclude from this reaction that Flannery was somehow being "open-minded" about sins related to sexuality, since that adjective usually implies a willingness to discard Church teachings. Nowhere in her letters does Flannery suggest to Hester that homosexuality is not sinful (in a 1954 letter to another friend, Flannery describes lesbianism as a "form of uncleanness"); instead, she always emphasizes that, like any other sin, it could be forgiven. If Flannery had wanted to condemn Hester, she could have stopped writing to her and stopped inviting her to Andalusia. Instead, she showed her friend mercy, just as Jesus did to the woman who had committed the sin of adultery

Speculations about Flannery's Sexuality

Over the years there has been plenty of speculation about Flannery's own sexuality. Since she never married and since she and Hester were such good friends, some modern secular critics have tried to brand their relationship as homosexual. These people might have suspected that the letters from Flannery to Hester that Sally Fitzgerald omitted from *The Habit of Being* would prove just this point. However, this cache of unpublished letters shows no signs of such a relationship. In fact, after he had read them, retired English professor William Sessions, who knew both women very well, did his best to put an end to rumors about the women's relationship. On May 10, 2007, Sessions was quoted in the newspaper as saying that "Betty had a crush on Flannery in the early years, but she seemed to be able to leave that behind as the friendship grew."[30] He was adamant that the letters reveal a caring relationship that was in no way romantic.

The rumors about the women's relationship, however, have persisted, as evidenced by a front-page article in the same newspaper about two years later. Commenting on Brad Gooch's newly released biography of Flannery, the *Atlanta Journal-Constitution* writer Bo Emerson said Gooch had pointed out that Flannery had attracted "unrequited crushes" from female admirers, including Hester. However, Emerson noted that Gooch's biography showed that she "otherwise lived a mostly monastic life, her libido channeled into her work." Still, rather inflammatory words appear in that same article, when Emerson opines that "speculations about O'Connor's sexuality" will continue to fuel interest in her life."[31]

"Love and Admiration"

Nowhere in the letters do we find evidence that Flannery suspected Hester had a crush on her. It is, of course, possible that the reason Hester had said she wanted to stop writing to Flannery, and to stop visiting Andalusia, had something to do with Hester's romantic feelings, but this is pure speculation. In any event, in the same letter in which Flannery alludes to Hester's past, she goes on to assure her friend that she is still welcome at Andalusia. She also promises to keep Hester's past a secret, especially from Regina, who, she said, was more easily shocked and who lived "in a world that Jane Austen would have been comfortable in." The letter ended on a very compassionate note: "I can see now how very much grace you have really been given. That is all that is necessary for me to know in the matter." She assured her friend of her "very real love and admiration."[32]

Hester's secret came up again in a postscript to a letter dated November 29, 1956, which appears in *The Habit of Being*. In it Flannery attempted to assure Hester again that the past was over and done with. Evidently Hester had turned down an invitation to Andalusia, which distressed Flannery, prompting her to write, "I wish you could come but I respect your reasons." She also corrected her earlier remark that Hester was different from her history: "Perhaps what I should have said is that you are more than your history." Flannery acknowledged that even if we can't change who we fundamentally are, our nature is "put to a different use when a conversion occurs and of course it requires vigilance to put it to the proper use."[33]

Quail with a Purgatorial Look

The friendship between the two women continued, as did Hester's journey with Catholicism, and on June 10, 1957, Hester was confirmed[34] with Flannery serving as her sponsor by proxy. Five days after the ceremony, Flannery wrote Hester about seeing a list of sponsors and proxies in the Catholic newspaper, where Flannery had been listed as Mary F. O'Connor, which, she noted dryly, sounded "like somebody's washerwoman."[35] She sent her newly confirmed friend one of her original paintings, which depicted a quail with a "rather purgatorial look." In her typical deadpan fashion, Flannery added that she had wanted to send her friend a "pious article," but such things turned her stomach.[36]

"Everything That I Am Not"

Sadly, Hester's religious doubts came back to haunt her, and she apparently described her struggles in her letters to Flannery. As February opened in 1961, Flannery wrote to assure her that conversion was an ongoing journey. She described conversion as a deepening of faith, rather than an event that happened "once and for all and that's that." Conversion, she told Hester, meant continually turning toward God and away from egocentricity. For this to happen, "You have to see this selfish side of yourself in order to turn from it." She reminded Hester that everyone falls short, and in her typical humble fashion, she included herself: "I measure God by everything that I am not."[37]

In the fall of 1961, Hester wrote Flannery to tell her the very sad news: she had left the Catholic Church. Not surprisingly, this confession greatly distressed Flannery and her mother as well, and in her response, Flannery admitted frankly, "I don't know anything that could grieve us here like this news." As disappointed as she was, Flannery refrained from passing judgment on her friend, remarking that "I know that what you do you do because you think it is right." She also assured Hester that their friendship would continue, since she would think no less of her "outside the Church than in it."[38]

Despite these reassuring words, Flannery was not going to sidestep the deeper truth. And thus, in that same letter, she told Hester what it meant to leave the Catholic Church. "What is painful is the realization that this means a narrowing of life for you and a lessening of the desire for life."[39]

Hester's Low Self-Esteem

Flannery was understandably distressed about her friend's loss of faith. As she told Hester, some people who lose faith in Christ go on to "substitute a swollen faith in themselves." She admitted that she didn't think this would happen in Hester's case, since Hester evidently struggled with a lack of self-confidence. However, Flannery feared that Hester's already low self-esteem was in danger of worsening: "Now that you don't believe in Christ, you will believe even less in yourself; which in itself is regrettable."[40]

She also advised Hester to be steadfast in her will, and not put too much stock in the feelings of the moment. Faith fluctuates, Flannery assured her friend: "It rises and falls like the tides of an invisible ocean." And she expressed hope that the tide would turn for Hester in the future. Her words were gentle, but again she didn't shy away from stating the truth: leaving the Church would not solve Hester's problems. However, Flannery also wanted to remind her friend that she could always return: "All I can suggest to you, as your one-time sponsor, is that if you find in yourself the least return of a desire for faith, to go back to the Church... without the conscience-raking to which you are probably subject."[41]

Finding Christ

When Hester's letter didn't arrive on Monday as it usually did, Flannery became concerned. Writing on November 11, 1961, Flannery admitted her fear that "she's thrown out the Church and now she's going to throw me out with it." It seems that Hester's feelings had been hurt, but Flannery was quick to make amends. "I hadn't meant to imply that you felt any guilt over leaving," she wrote. "I think your idea of why you left is ingenious," she added, although she didn't specify what that reason was.[42]

Hester apparently had told Flannery that she was starting to like herself the way she was. In Flannery's eyes, this change of attitude was a grace that had nonetheless come from the Church. Indeed, she suggested that this newfound self-esteem might be the "first step toward finding the Church again." Flannery also said Hester one day might wonder why she spent so much time in self-reflection. In these remarks, Flannery revealed a crucial insight about her own relationship with Christ. She suggested that we must empty our hearts of selfishness to make room for him: "You will have found Christ when you are concerned with other people's sufferings and not your own."[43]

In fact, at the time she wrote this letter, the symptoms related to lupus had so debilitated her that she had been using crutches for six years. Yet nowhere in the letters do we find her complaining about her headaches, rashes, and extreme fatigue, her swollen and painful joints, the sensitivity to light, the hair loss, the ulcers in her mouth. Nowhere in this letter does she point to herself as one of those who have "found" Christ. Her letters show her to be more concerned with Hester's suffering than her own, and this is a grace that comes from God.

Abandonment of Self

"Oh dear" was the plaintive opening to Flannery's next letter. Apparently her comments about finding Christ had offended Hester. "It had not occurred to me that you didn't feel for people," she explained, adding that she was thinking of something "a good deal more radical." She reiterated a point from her other letters: Feelings were not that important in matters of faith. "The kind of concern I mean is a doing, not a feeling,"[44] she said, referring to the will triumphing over emotions.

To make amends, she put herself in the same proverbial boat with Hester. She said that a victory of the will comes from grace, "which neither you nor I... in the remotest sense possesses." As an example of a grace-filled woman, she mentioned Sister Evangelist, who cheerfully cared for dying cancer patients in Atlanta. This sister, whom Flannery deeply admired, exemplified "abandonment of self" which came from the gift of sanctifying grace.[45]

"Now You Can See"

There was some sparring between the two friends in future letters. Apparently Hester had chafed at Flannery's suggestion that losing faith in Christ meant having less faith in herself. "I see that I was wrong," Flannery wrote cynically: "Faith is blindness and now you can see." Dropping the caustic tone, she went on to encourage Hester's latest writing plan, which involved taking off six months from her job: "You will be able now to do anything you want — the novel or criticism... and believe me, nobody will rejoice in this like I will – not the heresy but in the success."[46] Although Flannery did not name the "heresy" at that point, she noted in a letter to their mutual friend Cecil Dawkins, a female author and professor at Stephens College in Missouri, that "She doesn't believe any longer that Christ is God." [47]

"Pretty Sick Making"

It also seems that Hester was developing a new fascination. According to William Sessions, she had become interested in the work of British author Iris Murdoch, and she would write to her for many years.[48] In her letter to Dawkins, Flannery opined that their friend's attraction to Murdoch, an atheist, was implicated in Hester's loss of faith. She told Dawkins somewhat bitterly that although Hester no longer believed in Christ's divinity, "She has found that he is 'beautiful! beautiful!'" She added darkly: "The effect of all this on me is pretty sick-making but I manage to keep my mouth shut."[49]

In that letter to Dawkins, Flannery reiterated the point she had made earlier to Hester: if Christ was not God, he was not beautiful, but "merely pathetic." She also sounded a warning about Hester, which sadly would come true in the future:

> She is now against all intellectualism. She thinks she's at last discovered how to be herself and has at last accepted herself. She says she's always tried to be someone else because she hated herself, but now she can be herself. It's as plain as the nose on

her face that now she's being Iris Murdoch, but it is only plain to me, not her. What I am afraid of is that the reaction is going to set in in a couple of months, or maybe not that soon, but sometime, and when it does BANG. Everything runs to extremes with her as you can see.[50]

On January 26, 1962, Flannery wrote Dawkins again and mentioned that Hester's initial enthusiasm for the Church had worn off after only five years. "She hadn't penetrated far enough to be able to do without it," Flannery said. "She must always be emotionally involved."[51]

A few weeks earlier, still upset about her spiritual protégée leaving the Church, Flannery had expressed dismay to Hester about her poor grasp of important Catholic teachings. "You confuse self-abandonment in the Christian sense with a refusal to be yourself, with self-torture." She tried to set Hester straight about the difference between self-hatred and surrendering self to Christ: "Self-torture is abnormal; asceticism is not." As for losing a sense of self, she claimed that writing would help, citing an example from her own experience: "I never completely forget myself except when I'm writing and I am never more completely myself except when I am writing. It is the same thing with Christian self-abandonment."[52]

Elation and Depression

Poor Hester suffered from manic depression, a problem alluded to in the letters following her exit from the Church. On February 10, 1962, Flannery admitted to Hester that she worried about her, but she had no advice for "these up and down times of elation & depression." She warned her friend that "time is very dangerous without a rigid routine."[53] Her concern about Hester's moodiness continued, and a month later, she noted to Dawkins that their mutual friend was very lethargic. She also expressed worry over Hester's comment about being nearly thirty-nine "and not able to learn new tricks." She told Dawkins that they needed to do something to cheer up Hester.[54]

Writing to Hester in mid-March, Flannery addressed the emotional problem head-on: "I really hadn't realized the extent to which your recent exhilaration-depression was in the neighborhood of a nervous breakdown." Hester had by this time returned to her job, a move that Flannery applauded, because this meant less time for brooding. As for Hester's loss of faith, she said: "That is only fatal if you have lost the desire for it."[55]

Falling Down the Drain of Relativism

Flannery had little patience with moral relativism. She believed in truth with a capital T, and she found that truth in Catholicism. On May 19, 1962, Flannery reacted darkly to Hester's evident fascination with relativism by writing, "It is my duty to worship and worship only what I believe to be true." She referred to Hester's apparent embrace of relativism as a belief that "it-doesn't-make-any-difference-what-but-only-how [you worship]." She minced no words, calling this "a drain down which I hate to see you falling."[56] Although it is clear from a letter written about a year later that the two were still good friends – Hester had just visited Andalusia and left candy as a gift – Flannery was terse when it came to Hester's views on right and wrong. "Your views on morality are for never-never land," she said flatly. "We don't live in it."[57]

Suffering of Christ

Although Hester no longer believed in Christ's divinity, this didn't stop her spiritual director from affirming her own deep faith in subsequent letters. Writing on October 26, 1963, Flannery alluded to a problem that Hester must have grappled with, that is, a feeling of being unloved and misunderstood. Flannery interpreted such emotional suffering in light of her Catholic faith: "It all comes under the larger heading of what individuals have to suffer for the common good, a mystery, and part of the suffering of Christ."[58]

Despite their not seeing eye-to-eye on faith, the friendship between the two women remained strong. Flannery continued to encourage her friend's writing efforts and shared her own stories with her. Hester's visits to Andalusia to see Flannery and Regina continued. And when Andalusia's resident burro, Ernest, became a father, Flannery proudly sent her friend photos. The correspondence between the two friends continued until a few weeks before Flannery's death in 1964.

✠   ✠   ✠   ✠

Hester's life ended on a very tragic note. According to Sessions, her final years were marked by serious physical decline, and toward the end, she worried that she was losing control of her body. In 1998, on the day after Christmas, Hester died at age seventy-six from a self-inflicted gunshot wound. She died all alone among her thousands of books.[59]

If Flannery were alive today, she would probably dismiss the idea that she was a "spiritual director" to Hester, thinking the title too highfalutin and preferring simply to be called Hester's "friend." It is clear from the letters that she was indeed a devoted friend, to a woman who, as our glimpses of Hester suggest, was not easy to befriend: a woman who at times was melancholy, needy, and somewhat narcissistic. But even if Flannery might not like the title, she was undeniably a powerful spiritual model and guide for her friend – patient in teaching and nonjudgmental in support. Flannery clearly was delighted when Hester converted to the Catholic faith, since that made the spiritual tie between the two women even closer. But she certainly wouldn't have taken credit for the conversion, since she herself was such a believer in the mysterious gift of God's grace. She was mystified when her friend left the Church, and bitterly disappointed, but she remained hopeful that Hester would one day return.

In any event, Flannery remained Hester's friend over nine years and through 274 letters, showing her abiding charity over the years as she tried to help her weather her turbulent stream of emotional highs and lows. Flannery was a friend in the truest sense of the word, trying to counter Hester's self-hatred and encouraging her when she became despondent. Her prediction that, without grounding in Catholicism, Hester's self-hatred would intensify sadly came true in 1998, when Hester took her own life.

But Flannery could not have predicted how wrongly the world would misjudge the deep affection the two women had for one another. Hester may possibly have had a crush on Flannery, but from the guilt and remorse alluded to in the letters it seems clear that Hester was committed to overcoming her sexual feelings for women. Unfortunately, the secular world continues to overlook the spiritual and emotional dimension of their friendship.

In a 1960 letter to William Sessions, Flannery lamented the kind of critical reading "that sees in every door handle a phallic symbol," and puts questionable intentions in the minds of authors "who have other fish to fry."[60] We can imagine her leveling the same charge at modern critics who try to sexualize her friendship with Betty Hester. An inscription in a book that Flannery gave her pen pal nicely sums up their relationship, reading simply, "To Betty Hester, my adopted kin." Indeed, Flannery, in her steadfast, faithful friendship, had "other fish to fry."

CHAPTER 4

Escape from Nihilism: The Sagas of Alfred Corn and Roslyn Barnes

The heart of Christianity is based on the new command-ment that Jesus gave his disciples in John 13:34: "Love one another even as I have loved you." Jesus uttered this com-mandment shortly after he had washed the disciples' feet. This is one of the most stunning and vivid images in the New Testa-ment: God stooping in servitude towards his creatures. The scene reminds us that following Christ will not be easy. We can attend weekly liturgy, fast on the prescribed days, donate money to good causes, and live the Ten Commandments by the book. But without a true conversion of heart, without the willingness to serve others, a Christian is in danger of falling into complacency.

Fortunately, the lives of some everyday Christians give us a glimpse at an effort to truly practice Christ-like, selfless love. This effort is evident in Flannery's letters. In her cor-respondence Flannery did not wax poetic about self-sacrifice;

rather she modeled it by generously giving the one thing that she had little of, which was her time. She couldn't "wash feet" by working in a soup kitchen or visiting the sick. Her own diminished physical energy limited her writing time to about two hours each morning, yet she still put great effort into letters to people seeking spiritual advice. In addition to Hester, who became a good friend, Flannery also corresponded with two others whom she barely knew. One was Alfred Corn, a young poet who had heard one of her talks at Emory University in 1962, and the other was Roslyn Barnes, a student at the State University of Iowa.

Breathing in Nihilism

Corn was attending college at a time when it was fashionable to ride the coattails of Friedrich Nietzsche, who claimed that God was dead, and Jean-Paul Sartre, who described life as meaningless. "If you live today you breathe in nihilism," Flannery had written to Hester, seven years earlier. "It's the gas you breathe."[1] Flannery herself knew plenty about this particular poisonous gas; for in her short story "Good Country People," she had created the character of Hulga, a highly educated nihilist who was spiritually as well as physically crippled.

Hulga stands as one of Flannery's most scathing indictments of secular college education. She has a Ph.D. in philosophy and is thirty-two years old, but is unemployed and living at home with her mother. A large blonde with an artificial leg, Hulga had her name legally changed from Joy when she was away at college, largely to annoy her mother, Mrs. Hopewell. At college Hulga also became an atheist, and she prides herself on believing in nothing until she meets her match in the aptly named Manley Pointer, a young Bible salesman.

Alone with her in the barn, Pointer lures her into saying that she loves him, and then kisses her. It soon becomes apparent, however, that he is the real nihilist, keeping condoms and whiskey in his hollowed-out Bible, and roaming the countryside collecting bizarre trophies (for example, glass eyes) from unsuspecting women. His goal is not sex but humiliation, and he achieves it by stealing Hulga's wooden leg. His parting words to her are, "I been believing in nothing ever since I was born."

"Help My Unbelief"

The story appears in the collection *A Good Man Is Hard to Find*, and was published in 1955, so it's possible that Corn had read it when he first wrote to Flannery in 1962. We don't have that initial letter, unfortunately, but it is easy to imagine its contents. He probably told her a bit about his Christian upbringing, before confiding that his college courses seemed to be whittling away at his faith. Many years later, Corn described his reason for writing that letter: "I had seen, over the previous year, the Protestant fundamentalism of my upbringing crumble away from me under the flood of new ideas proposed in various undergraduate courses." After hearing Flannery talk in one of his classes, he wrote to her to find out how she "with her sharp and cultivated mind, had retained her faith."[2]

In her first reply, written on May 30, 1962, Flannery tried to reassure him. The very fact that he was worried about his faith, she said, proved that he had some left. She also reminded him of the plea made to Jesus in Mark 9:24: "Lord, I believe. Help my unbelief." This cry, she said, was the most natural, human, and agonizing prayer in the Gospels: "I think it is the foundation prayer of faith."[3]

Since his arrival at college, Corn had been bombarded with secular ideas – especially, it seems, the relativistic claims of "comparative religion" – and he found himself unprepared for the battle. He was just beginning, as Flannery said, "to realize how difficult it is to have faith and the measure of commitment to it." As for his fear that he'd had lost his faith, she told him in no uncertain terms, "You are too young to decide you don't have faith just because you feel you can't believe." Echoing her comments to Hester, she pointed out the danger of measuring faith by feelings: what counts, she said, is what we actually do.[4]

Looking for God in Other Ways

Like many young people, Corn needed assurance that he was not alone in his struggles, and Flannery came to his rescue. "Students get so bound up with difficulties such as reconciling the clashing of so many different faiths such as Buddhism, Mohammedanism, etc.," she told him, "that they cease to look for God in other ways."[5]

To exemplify seeking God in other ways, she mentioned an exchange between the poets Robert Bridges and Gerard Manley Hopkins. When Bridges wrote Hopkins for advice on believing in God, Hopkins did not reply with a long philosophical answer. Instead, he wrote back, "Give alms." Flannery explained that we can find God by performing charitable acts, that is, we can find God by loving the divine image in human beings. "Don't get so entangled with intellectual difficulties that you fail to look for God in this way."[6]

Her actions here reflect her own charitable heart. Although she had never met Corn, she gave him a great deal of attention in her letters, and even invited him to visit her at Andalusia. She also confided that she had once experienced the same problems during her own college days: "At one time, the clash of the different world religions was a difficulty for me. Where you have absolute solutions, however, you have no need of faith." As she so aptly defined it, faith is "what you have in the absence of knowledge."[7]

Christian Skepticism

Skepticism is usually associated with resisting faith, but Flannery had a different take on the matter: "What kept me a sceptic [sic] in college was precisely my Christian faith." By this she meant that her faith helped her avoid jumping to conclusions, by saying, "Wait, don't bite on this, get a wider picture, continue to read." She advised Corn to adopt this same skepticism. For every anti-Christian book that he read, for instance, she recommended reading one that showed the other side of the story. "To find out about faith, you have to go to the people who have it." She urged him to read books by the most intelligent people of faith so he could hold his own with "agnostics and the general run of pagans that you are going to find in the majority of people around you."[8] This Christian skepticism, she said, would keep him free: "Not free to do anything you please, but free to be formed by something larger than your own intellect or the intellects of those around you."[9]

Relativism of Protestants

As we saw earlier, Hester had struggled with the notion that religious faith is opposed to reason, and Corn also may have suffered from this false dilemma. In a letter dated June 16, 1962, Flannery emphasized to the young man that the Catholic Church does not require the death of reason. On the contrary, she said bluntly, "If what the Church teaches is not true, then the security and emotional release and sense of purpose it gives you are of no value and you are right to reject it."[10]

She went on to take some swipes at "modern liberal Protestantism," which she claimed had made truth vaguer and increasingly relative. She also criticized Protestants for banishing intellectual distinctions and relying on feeling instead of thought. Since Protestants lack a central authority to make decisions on faith and morals, she said, religion became their "own sweet invention." She gently put it to Corn, a Protestant, that "This seems to be about where you find yourself now."

It is worth emphasizing that Flannery's disagreement was with *liberal* Protestants, not with the more conservative branches. As a Catholic she found much more in common with the traditional doctrines and scriptural fidelity of fundamentalist Protestants, which partly explains why the latter run rampant throughout her stories. In her way of thinking, the fundamentalists had retained a good deal of Catholic belief. They continued to believe in the reality of the devil, the existence of sin, and the divinity of Christ. As she explained it in a letter to Sister Mariella Gable, "Theologically our differences with them are on the nature of the Church, not on the nature of God or our obligation to him."[11] As for liberal Protestants, in her letter to Corn she criticized them for banishing intellectual distinctions and relying on feeling instead of thought.

Conversely, the Catholic faith emphasizes finding God through reason, as well as revelation. As she had also told Hester, she emphasized to Corn that not only was there was no need to shut off the intellect to embrace Catholic teachings, but in fact the intellect can be made to serve faith: "I believe what the Church teaches – that God has given us reason to use and that it can lead us toward a knowledge of him."[12]

Does Free Will Exist?

Free will was evidently another hot topic in Corn's college classes. Growing up in a Christian home, he would have been taught about man's freedom to choose between right and wrong. In college, however, he was learning about psychologists who claimed that free will didn't exist. He apparently was wondering: If people weren't free, could they really be capable of sin? If they couldn't make truly free choices, why would God punish or reward people for their actions?

Flannery set him straight. On August 12, 1962, she wrote to him about her characters Rayber and Tarwater, from her novel *The Violent Bear It Away*. Responding to a remark made by Corn, she emphasized that neither one exhibited a lack of free will. "An absence of free will in these characters would mean an absence of conflict in them, whereas they spend all their time fighting within themselves, drive against drive."[13]

In this letter, she rejected the notion of determinism, although she did admit that certain actions, such as those of a psychotic, could not really be called free. She went on to point out that, according to Catholic teaching, God does not judge such actions, nor does he predestine any soul to hell – a belief that she called a "Protestant phenomenon."[14] Here she refers to the passage in Romans 9, which she says Luther and Calvin interpreted as proof for predestination, a doctrine that the Catholic Church has always condemned. The Church's official teaching on this passage, she points out, is that it refers not to predestination but to the different talents and gifts that God gives people in their earthly lives. On a more personal note, she added that even literature would be impossible in a world where people lacked free will: a writer "might go through the motions but the heart would be out of it." Writing two novels had taught her that "the more you write, the less inclined you will be to rely on theories like determinism."[15]

"Christ Speaking in Time"

Corn evidently was curious about decision-making in the Catholic Church. In that same letter, dated August 12, Flannery explained a key belief of her faith: after Christ established his Church on earth, he did not abandon it. Instead, he continues to speak to the flock through the shepherd on earth, the pope. "It is the Bishops, not priests, who decide religious questions in the Catholic Church,"[16] with the pope, as bishop of Rome, having the final authority. She also explained very cogently the Catholic doctrine of papal infallibility: "Catholics believe that Christ left the Church with a teaching authority [that is] protected by the Holy Ghost." This means that in teaching on matters of faith and morals the Church cannot make mistakes: "She is Christ speaking in time."[17]

Flannery's words might have surprised Corn, who was being taught in college always to think for himself. She assured him, however, that in telling her what was true and false regarding faith, and right and wrong regarding morals, the Church wasn't infringing on her intellectual independence. "Certainly I am no fit judge," she explained. "If left to myself, I certainly wouldn't know how to interpret Romans IX." We see an instance of what Flannery considered the do-it-yourself Protestant approach to biblical interpretation in *Wise Blood,* where Hoover Shoates tries to promote his own church by proclaiming, "You can sit at home and interprit your own Bible however you feel in your heart it ought to be interprited." For Flannery, such a purely subjective approach to interpreting Scripture – the Protestant's Principle of Private Judgment – clashed with the Catholic belief in absolute truth. As she told Corn, "I don't believe Christ left us to chaos."[18]

"You Become *a Catholic"*

Like Corn, Roslyn Barnes was a non-Catholic, but she was on a very different path from the Emory student. She was studying at Georgia State College for Women in Milledgeville when she first sought out Flannery, but it was when Barnes went on to study science and writing in Iowa City that she began writing Flannery about her interest in Catholicism. In an early letter dated December 12, 1960, Flannery began laying the groundwork for the girl's conversion.

First she explained the big difference between Catholic and Protestant conversion experiences: "You don't join the Catholic Church. You *become* a Catholic."[19] Accordingly, over time, Flannery did not just write to Barnes; she also opened her home to the girl, and enlisted others to pray for her.

Parents Raising a Ruckus

Barnes was not, as Corn was, besieged by intellectual doubts. In fact, she was well on her way to accepting Catholic teachings, so Flannery did not have to explain fine theological distinctions to her. Instead, in her December 12 letter, Flannery recommended a trio of practices for Barnes, explaining that studying dogma would help her intellectually, while praying and attending Mass would prepare her entire personality for conversion.

Sadly, the girl faced a big barrier on her journey, as her parents were adamantly opposed to Catholicism and dead-set against her conversion. "I wish that there were a book that you could give your parents that would prepare them for your interest," Flannery wrote, "because... you should at least try to cushion the blow if you are going to give them one."[20] On January 23, 1961, Flannery expressed further sympathy for the girl, whose parents were continuing to raise a "ruckus." Rather than arguing with them, though, Flannery suggested that Barnes pray for them.[21]

Supporting the Troops

Prayer, study, and Mass worked wonders for Flannery's protégée. On July 26, 1961, Flannery told Barnes she would be delighted to recommend her for the Papal Auxiliary Volunteers for Latin America. It seems the girl had not only been received into the Church, but also was contemplating becoming a nun. And although there is no mention of the parents' reactions, we can assume they were none too thrilled.

Flannery proved just as full of practical advice as spiritual, applauding Barnes for trying volunteer work "before you even think about becoming a Sister," and advising her to pay off her college loans. She added, very kindly, that although many people might not understand the girl's wanting to become a missionary, "I think it is fine."[22] About a year later, Barnes was teaching catechism as a papal volunteer in Cuernavaca, Mexico, with Flannery continuing to cheer her on. She asked the girl if the other volunteers needed anything: "Just let me know what I can do to support the troops."[23]

"Remember Her"

On August 5, 1962, Flannery wrote Father McCown about her "convert friend" in Mexico. She sent the priest one of the girl's letters, asking him to pray for her. There is no indication of what prompted this request, but Flannery might have felt that Barnes was in danger. "Send me the letter back but remember her," she wrote. Describing Barnes as a very bright convert "with a real vocation," she also gave Father McCown an update on the parents, who, unfortunately, remained "violently opposed" to the girl's endeavors.[24] Showing great kindness to Barnes, Flannery wrote a few weeks later to let her know that this priest was praying for her.[25]

Three months later, Barnes had returned to the U.S., but family tensions were running so high that the girl spent a week at Andalusia rather than visiting her parents. After that, she planned to leave for Valparaiso, Chile, to teach chemistry at a Jesuit university. Writing to Father McCown on November 2, 1962, Flannery commented sadly, "The poor girl really has no home." She also expressed concern about Barnes's teaching chemistry in Spanish, saying the girl knew about as much of the language as a three-year-old. "Lord help us all" was the conclusion to this letter.[26]

Mystical Types

Flannery's bemused description of one of Barnes' visits to Andalusia seems like a scene from one of her stories. "My mother does not suffer mystical types gladly,"

Flannery told Hester. Evidently the girl had gone outdoors to admire nature, and Regina had discovered her
lying flat on the ground in the fifty-degree weather. "Can't
you look at things standing up?" Regina asked, admonish-
ing Barnes either to get up or catch her death of cold. "It's
so much more sacramental to lie on the ground," Barnes
replied. "In two days she had a cold," Flannery remarked
wryly to Hester. "You can't get ahead of mother."[27]

The little glimpses we get of Roslyn in Flannery's
letters unfortunately do not add up to a clear-cut por-
trait of this young woman, but the patchwork of remarks
provides insights into the woman from whom she sought
advice. We learn, for example, that Flannery felt comfortable enough with Roslyn to admit her misgivings about a
direction in which the Church was heading in 1961, a year
before the Second Vatican Council was convened. In one
letter, Flannery tells Roslyn that she forgot her missal
at Mass one day and used a paper one that she found in
the pew. "The Latin in it had been translated to make it
appealing to idiots," Flannery complained, "everything in
baby-English, enough to turn your stomach." Later she
added, "So many of these attempts to get the Mass nearer
the participants are misdirected."[28]

In another letter to Roslyn, written in August,
1962, Flannery mentioned that the girl was in a "school
for sanctity," which no doubt referenced her studying to
become a nun. Writing about the monsignor who was
in charge, Flannery opined that he would not be able
to create saints in four months, "but he has to try." She
also sounded a note of approval for Roslyn, assuring
her that even if half the class didn't make it, Roslyn
certainly would. Flannery went on to say that "This
is surely what it means to bear away the kingdom of
heaven with violence."

She does not cite the Scripture passage from which that reference comes, but it is Matthew 11:12: "From the days of John the Baptist until now the kingdom of heaven has suffered violence, and men of violence take it by force." Flannery suggested to Roslyn that the meaning of this passage is that "the violence is directed inward."[29] Although she did not elaborate, it seems that she was referring to the internal pruning of vices and sinful inclinations that Roslyn – and any serious Christian – must be diligent about.

✠   ✠   ✠   ✠

Alfred Corn graduated from Emory with a degree in French literature and went on to become a well-known poet and essayist. Although he never accepted Flannery's invitation to visit her at Andalusia, he never forgot her generosity in writing to him. Over thirty-five years later, he expressed his appreciation, saying that he admired her willingness to answer his questions and to grapple with "what is difficult and apparently insoluble in human efforts to comprehend the divine."[30]

Roslyn Barnes's fate was far more mysterious. We know that Flannery was worried about the girl when she became a missionary, and that she asked Father McCown to pray for Barnes, although we are not told what the source of Flannery's concern was. In a magazine article published in 1979, about fifteen years after Flannery's death, Father McCown recalled Barnes as a "brilliant girl" who had converted to Catholicism with Flannery's encouragement. He described Barnes as "Catholic with a vengeance," citing her enthusiasm in becoming a papal volunteer. After they were introduced by mail, he and Barnes kept in touch, although they never met.

After Flannery's death, he asked Barnes for the letters she had received from Flannery, and some of these ended up in *The Habit of Being*. Father McCown also contacted the girl's mother, who had not heard from her daughter since 1968.[31] It is possible that she met a tragic and perhaps violent end during the course of her missionary work in South America. According to Fitzgerald, who was writing in 1979, efforts to find out what had happened to the girl proved fruitless.[32]

The letters in *The Habit of Being* stand as a shining testimony to this young life. In the very last one, dated August 26, 1962, Flannery asked Roslyn if she would be visiting Andalusia in October. "Remember," she told the girl, "that anytime you are welcome."[33] Perhaps more than anything, this invitation to Andalusia remains a beautiful witness to the friendship that had grown between Barnes and Flannery. Yes, Flannery provided spiritual guidance to the girl, and likely helped along her conversion. But, more than that, Flannery revealed her dedication to putting into practice Christ's dictum to "love one another as I have loved you." She showed the girl Christ-like love by welcoming her to her "abbey" and by praying for her.

III

A Ministry of Writing

"When you get well," she said, "I think it would be nice if you wrote a book about down here.

We need another good book like *Gone with the Wind*."

He could feel the muscles in his stomach begin to tighten.

"Put the war in it," she advised. "That always makes a long book."

He put his head back gently as if he were afraid it would crack. After a moment he said, "I am not going to write any book."

"Well," she said, "if you don't feel like writing a book, you could just write poems. They're nice."

—*"The Enduring Chill"*

·CHAPTER 5·

A "Genuine Miracle": Memoir of Mary Ann

*T*oo often, the media portray religious sisters as strict women in black garb with dreary expressions. The Dominican Sisters of Hawthorne, a joyful religious order with which Flannery had a strong spiritual connection, easily belied this stereotype. Some of these sisters ran – and to this day still run – Our Lady of Perpetual Help Home for incurable cancer patients in Atlanta, which opened in 1939. When Hester discovered in 1956 that one of the sisters there was an ex-dancer, she was quite surprised; Flannery, however, wasn't shocked at all. Indeed, she replied calmly that this was "just another indication of the Grace that must move through that place." She then added a very strong vote of confidence in the Dominican sisters: "I have more admiration for them than any other order I know." [1]

Little did Flannery realize, when she wrote these words, that she soon would be earning the sisters' admiration as well.

Unique Style of Preaching

The Dominican Sisters of Hawthorne were founded in 1900 by Rose Hawthorne Lathrop, daughter of writer Nathaniel Hawthorne and a convert to Catholicism. While living in New York she had been deeply moved by the tragic plight of impoverished cancer patients, whom most people avoided as if they were lepers. Those who could not afford hospital treatment often were left on their own to die or sent to Blackwell's Island, the last refuge for New York's penniless, located in the East River and today known as Roosevelt's Island. "In either case," Flannery noted, "it was a matter of being left to rot."[2]

In the fall of 1896, after taking a three-month nursing course, Lathrop found an apartment in the Lower East Side of Manhattan where she began giving free care to the dying poor. Joined in her efforts by artist Alice Huber and other women, Lathrop took her vows as a Dominican nun on Dec. 8, 1900. Huber also took vows, becoming Sister Mary Rose, and together they founded the Dominican Congregation of St. Rose of Lima, later called the Servants of Relief for Incurable Cancer.[3] Lathrop became Mother Mary Alphonsa, and today her nuns, called the Dominican Sisters of Hawthorne, still are nursing incurable cancer patients, free of charge, in three homes in the United States and one in Kenya.

Dominicans are known as the "Order of Preachers," but these sisters do not spread the Gospel of Jesus Christ with words delivered from a pulpit. Rather, they preach in their own unique fashion, through their actions at the bedsides of the dying. In their homes, the sisters tenderly bathe their patients, feed them, read to them, pray with them, and even tuck them into bed at night.

The humble sisters put into practice a deep-seated belief in the sanctity of life, while showing through their loving ministry that suffering is not meaningless. Especially today, in a world where euthanasia is suggested as a "solution" to suffering, the sisters' ministry fills a crucial niche. They are living the words of Jesus Christ in Matthew 25:40: "As you did it to one of the least of these my brethren, you did it to me."

The Saintly Child

Mary Ann Long was a little girl cared for by the Dominican sisters at Our Lady of Perpetual Help home, located in southwest Atlanta. They called her a "saintly child" when she came to them in 1949, when she was just three, and they looked after her until her death nine years later.[4] The sisters heard about Flannery through the monks at the Monastery of the Holy Spirit in Conyers, Georgia, and they wrote her in spring of 1960 to tell her about the child. Sister Evangelist, who was in charge of the home, explained that the poor girl had been born with a cancerous tumor on her face, which had grown so large that one of her eyes had been surgically removed. Despite her deformity and illness, however, the sisters had not considered the child afflicted. "After one meeting," the letter read, "one never was conscious of her physical defect but recognized only the beautiful brave spirit and felt the joy of such contact."[5]

On April 30, 1960, Flannery reported to Hester that Sister Evangelist had written her and had enclosed pictures of Mary Ann, along with a copy of the bishop's sermon delivered at the child's funeral. Sister's letter also contained a request for a very large favor: would Flannery be willing to write a story about the child – "fiction, or otherwise?" As Flannery later related to Hester, the sisters wanted the world to know about this saintly child. But Flannery replied to Sister that such a story shouldn't be fiction, nor was it the kind of thing she could write. She could have ended the matter then and there, but her charitable heart prevented her. She then suggested that the nuns compile their memories of Mary Ann and send them to her, and she would then do any editing that proved necessary. Also, if needed, she would write an introduction.[6]

Flinching Before Nothing

The abbot at the Monastery of the Holy Spirit, Cistercian Father Augustine Moore, was eager to discuss the proposed project with Flannery. He had visited the child at the cancer home and had been present at her funeral Mass. He also knew Flannery, since she and her mother had visited the monastery often, after their friend Tom Gossett took them there the first time.[7] In that same letter to Hester, Flannery mentioned that the abbot and Father Paul Bourne, also from the monastery, were slated to arrive at Andalusia the next day for lunch. She was beginning to worry about the consequences of her generous impulse: "Dear Lord knows what I will be in for."[8]

Little was decided at that meeting, but about three months later the Abbot returned, bringing with him Monsignor Dodwell and six of the sisters from the cancer home. It was during that visit that Flannery grew to admire the sisters more than ever; afterwards she described them as women who "flinched before nothing." There was, however, one awkward moment that day when one sister asked Flannery why she wrote about such strange characters – "why the grotesque (of all things) was my vocation." Flannery was struggling to get off the hook when another guest supplied the answer that would dispel the mystery, telling the sister, "It's your vocation, too."[9]

This startling comment opened up for Flannery what she called a "new perspective on the grotesque." In the introduction to the sisters' book, she noted that most of us, over time, are not very shocked by evil in the world; indeed, we may even become "dispassionate" about it. We "look it in the face and find, as often as not, our own grinning reflections." Good, she said, was quite another matter: few have stared at it long enough to see "that its face too is grotesque, that in us the good is something under construction." When we look into the face of goodness, she said, "We are liable to see a face like Mary Ann's, full of promise."[10]

Someone meeting Mary Ann for the first time might be so horrified by her deformed face that he'd be tempted to connect her cancer with the underlying grotesquerie of sin. But to Flannery this would be a terrible mistake, because even in physical evils like suffering and deformity, God makes his presence known. In Flannery's worldview, those who look with the eyes of faith can perceive "goodness in the making" even in suffering, because the deep promise in every person is the immortal soul. Looking at the Cross with Christ dying on it, the world might see only the terrible death of an innocent man, but the Christian recognizes "the good under construction," that is, the salvation of the world that resulted from the Cross.

"We've Had Some Demons"

One sister who took care of Mary Ann made a particularly strong impression on Flannery. It was the blue-eyed, bespectacled Sister Mary Evangelist Daly, whom Flannery described as "one of the funniest women I have ever encountered." On July 23, 1960, after the sisters' visit to Andalusia, Flannery avowed to Hester that Sister Evangelist possessed all the "rock-like qualities" necessary to minister to the incurably ill. Mary Ann's nurse, Sister Loretta, also was part of the entourage that day, along with three younger nuns. One of them Flannery frankly described as drawing very badly, while "the other two write (very, very badly)."[11]

Flannery could see that the sisters truly felt that the little girl had been a holy child. But she herself was at first reluctant to accept this opinion. For one thing, she figured any child raised by a group of nuns would probably display the kind of sweet piety that grated on her. When she mentioned this, however, Sister Evangelist disavowed her of that notion. "We've had some demons!"[12]

Before long, Flannery began to share the sisters' feelings about Mary Ann. As she told Hester, she became intrigued by "the mystery, the agony that is given in strange ways to children." Nonetheless she found it a strange and ironic twist that she was "about to write a book in collaboration with a convent."[13]

There is only one nun who makes an appearance in all of Flannery's stories, and she's a real jewel, calling to mind the big-hearted Sister Evangelist. In "A Temple of the Holy Ghost," a large, moon-faced nun welcomes a girl and her mother to the convent chapel by embracing the mother and then reaching out to the child. But the girl reacts coldly at first, extending her hand instead, because she looks down on the sisters who "kiss even homely children." During Benediction, however, the child's heart softens, and afterwards, the sister gets her hug. The child even lets the nun hold her a moment and look fondly at her with "little periwinkle eyes." This story came out in 1954, a few years before Flannery met the blue-eyed Sister Evangelist, so clearly the nun didn't inspire this scene, and yet the worlds of fiction and reality seem to mesh nicely here.

"She Don't Write Like Shakespeare"

Much to her relief, Flannery discovered that Sister Evangelist would be the one writing down the memories. And although Flannery confided to Hester that Sister "don't write like Shakespeare," she judged the nun up to the task. Later, as she learned more about the sisters' memories of Mary Ann, Flannery's intrigue grew, because she sensed the intense suffering the child had endured. The little girl had carried "an outsize cross and [bore] it with what most of us don't have and couldn't muster."[14]

In the fall of 1960, Flannery wrote to her editor, Robert Giroux, to tell him about Mary Ann and fill him in on the sisters' project. "The Sister Superior is determined that something must be written about her." She also admitted that after she advised the sisters to write the book themselves and offered to help them, she never expected to hear from them again. "Never underestimate them," she added wryly.[15] Once the sisters had compiled their memories of Mary Ann, they were "hellbent to see [the project] through." She added that Atlanta Bishop Francis Hyland, who evidently thought the child was a saint, also was interested in seeing the book take shape.

Obnoxious Pieties

Unfortunately, the sisters' manuscript was not very good. "There was everything about the writing to make the professional writer groan," Flannery complained.[16] She could detect that the sisters, in their unpolished fashion, had managed to convey the mystery of the child's life, but her editing task still seemed huge. She told Giroux that she had tried to remove the "obnoxious pieties" from the manuscript, but this had proved almost impossible. She asked him if he would read the manuscript once she edited it: "I know I can't make it into the kind of thing that you would publish but you might be able to tell me who might."[17]

Giroux graciously agreed to look at the edited manuscript, but a month later it still lay on her desk. This suggests that the editing was a much bigger job than she had anticipated. When a friend offered encouragement by declaring that the story was "moving," Flannery told Giroux flatly, "The only thing that moves me is the desire to get it off my desk."[18]

"Even Regina Liked It"

Flannery's emotions shifted as she began writing the introduction. "I have thought about it enough I suppose to make the writing of it a real pleasure," she admitted to Hester on November 12, 1960.[19] She planned to send Hester a draft and requested that she point out "when it begins to sound pompous." A few weeks later, Flannery reported to Hester that the sisters had read the draft and approved it. "Even Regina liked it which means something," she added, no doubt alluding to the fact that her mother often criticized her fiction.[20]

This letter reveals Flannery's heartfelt motivation for writing the introduction. As she was giving Hester advice on writing, Flannery noted, "You do not write the best you can for the sake of art but for the sake of returning your talent increased to the invisible God to use or not use as he sees fit."[21] She did not connect this "sermon," as she mockingly called it, with the introduction to the sisters' book. Still, it seems obvious that she herself was using her talent for a higher purpose, and although she didn't realize it at the time, the financial success of the book about Mary Ann would help the sisters carry out their ministry, bringing them – and their patients – great blessings.

"Dogs and Party Dresses"

It is little wonder that the sisters and Regina liked the introduction. Despite Flannery's initial reluctance to get involved in the project, her words remain a moving and deeply insightful reflection on human suffering. "One of the tendencies of our age is to use the suffering of children as a way to discredit God," she wrote, "and once you have discredited His goodness, you are done with Him."[22] Her words call to mind the image of an atheist pointing to an extremely deformed child like Mary Ann as evidence that God does not exist. One can hear the atheist booming, "Why in the world would a good God allow a child to suffer?"

The answer, of course, comes from looking at the big picture. As Flannery pointed out, it was true that the child's final days were filled with suffering, but her life was not a tragedy. In fact, the little girl thrived among the humble sisters. She also brought much mirth into the lives of the other patients at the cancer home. Although her own mother had left her at the home because she was too overwhelmed to deal with her, Mary Ann ended up with a whole flock of nuns to mother her. And despite their grim task of caring for the dying, the sisters were a cheery lot, and they thoroughly loved the little girl. When she'd arrived at the age of three, doctors had predicted she would die in six months, but she lived to be twelve. For those nine years, Sister Evangelist and her crew went all out. They provided the child with a puppy she called Scrappy, a parakeet, and a bevy of dolls. As Flannery described it, "Her days were full of dogs and party dresses, of Sisters and sisters, of Coca Colas and Dagwood sandwiches."[23]

When Flannery looked at Mary Ann's photos, she, like the nuns, saw much more than a severely deformed little girl. As Allen Pridgen has noted, Flannery recognized the sacramental element in all of life, and the child was no exception:

> In her introductory essay... O'Connor explains how she sees in the grotesqueness of Mary Ann's pain and death 'something full of promise,' 'the good under construction.' O'Connor's world... is a sacramental place full of signs, and human suffering is for her one of those signs that reveals that God has entered history in the Incarnation to redeem humankind through his love from what is otherwise *hopeless* suffering.[24]

This "something full of promise," of course, was the shining soul that the sisters also glimpsed in the child, and which the sisters at the home today continue to see in dying cancer patients.

Awe and Love

The world might think it impossible to find promise and joy in a cancer home, but many people have attested that the place where Mary Ann lived was – and still is – an upbeat place. In 1989, at the fiftieth anniversary celebration of Our Lady of Perpetual Help, reporter Gretchen Keiser described the atmosphere:

Decorations, blooming plants and homey touches mark the rooms. A second-floor porch furnished with white wrought iron furniture is bright with yellow cushions and large green plants. A venerable oak tree with a massive trunk stands in the back and shelters the yard, providing food for the eyes and the imagination. The nearby Atlanta Stadium is also a place of activity for patients to observe from the home or the gardens outside.[25]

At the celebration, Father Richard Lopez, chaplain at the home, described the sisters as "celibate... broke and working daily with the sick and dying," and praised them as the happiest people he had ever met. For many people, he said, the word "cancer" inspires fear and dread, but in the sisters' home, people encounter an atmosphere of love. Lopez, now a monsignor, had a simple and convincing explanation: "It's Jesus Christ." [26]

Laughter All Over the Building

Memories of Sister Evangelist, one of those particularly happy sisters, live on. In a recent letter, Mother Anne Marie Holden, the head of the Dominican Sisters of Hawthorne, recalled that Sister Evangelist "always had us laughing and best of all was that she could laugh at herself too." Mother added that the sisters at the cancer home always knew when Sister Evangelist was there "because they could hear her laughter all over the building."[27] No wonder Flannery admired her so much. Sister Evangelist clearly knew that Christ's loving sacrifice on the Cross had changed everything. As Allen Pridgen so beautifully put it, "The Passion of Christ... is the ultimate sacramental sign that shows how redemptive love can mysteriously exist in the face of innocent suffering and death."[28]

Joy in Suffering

"Innocent suffering" was a common denominator linking Flannery and Mary Ann Long. They both were stricken with chronic illnesses, and both were labeled "grotesque" in the eyes of the world. The child was terribly deformed by cancer, while Flannery was crippled by lupus. However, they both managed to find joy in the lives God had given them. Flannery had her faith and her writing, the birds and burros at Andalusia, her friends, and her beloved mother. Mary Ann had the sisters, her pets, her friends, and her self-created ministry of cheering up the cancer patients.

Mary Ann relied on the tender-hearted sisters for care, and Flannery was dependent on Regina; both had tender, affectionate relationships with their caretakers. Some critics have said in her stories – where mothers often are characterized negatively – Flannery would express hidden hostilities toward Regina. However, Father McCown, who knew mother and daughter well, disagreed with this theory. He recalled how Flannery strongly defended Regina as the widowed mother of an only child "whose physical health was her single-minded concern."[29] And even if Flannery and her mother often sparred with one another, Flannery's one great fear was that Regina would die before she did. "I don't know what I would do without her," she said.[30]

Charity Grows Invisibly

At Mary Ann's funeral, Bishop Francis E. Hyland made a very poignant remark. Many people might ask, he said, why such a friendly little girl had to die. Reflecting on his comment, Flannery said something that today seems darkly prophetic: "He could not have been thinking of that world... which would not ask why Mary Ann should die, but why she had been born in the first place."[31]

Today, that world is indeed energetically pursuing a course to rid humanity of flawed children like Mary Ann, using genetic testing to cull babies with genetic defects before birth. Medical science hails such measures as a gift to humanity; after all, will there not be fewer children suffering?

However, Cardinal Joseph Ratzinger, now Pope Benedict XVI, once noted that "Anyone who really wanted to get rid of suffering would have to get rid of love... because there can be no love without suffering, because it always demands an element of self-sacrifice."[32] Mary Ann knew little of theology, but if anyone had asked her, she surely would have expressed gratitude that despite her suffering she had been able to live a life that included friends, parties, and other expressions of love.

The Wretched Child

It is true that Mary Ann suffered, but Flannery did not believe she suffered in vain. Rather her suffering was a thread woven within the larger fabric of believers called the Communion of Saints. In the introduction, Flannery described the Communion of Saints as "the action by which charity grows invisibly among us, entwining the living and the dead."[33]

On May 14, 1961, she explained to a friend that "the living and the dead" referred to Nathaniel Hawthorne, who was her inspiration for the introduction.[34] Long before Mary Ann was born, Hawthorne had written about visiting the children's ward in a Liverpool workhouse. There, according to his description, he met a "wretched, pale, half-torpid" child of indeterminate sex, about six years old. Hawthorne admitted that he found the child repulsive, but for some mysterious reason, the child took a liking to him. The child insisted that Hawthorne pick him up. Despite his aversion, Hawthorne did what the child wanted: "I should never have forgiven myself if I had repelled its advances."[35]

According to Flannery, Mother Alphonsa believed that these were the greatest words her father ever wrote. And many years after Mother Alphonsa had died, Flannery perceived a mystical connection existing between Hawthorne's picking up the child, his daughter working among the dying, and the sisters caring for a little girl with a disfigured face.

> There is a direct line between the incident in the Liverpool workhouse, the work of Hawthorne's daughter, and Mary Ann – who stands not only for herself but for all the other examples of human imperfection and grotesquerie which the Sisters of Rose Hawthorne's order spend their lives caring for. Their work is the tree sprung from Hawthorne's small act of Christlikeness and Mary Ann its flower.[36]

"That's His Business"

Some skeptics might still say that a truly loving God would have healed Mary Ann. And so might some Christians – indeed, a self-styled faith healer had visited the child in the cancer home with just this thought in mind. "The Lord Jesus can heal you!" he bellowed repeatedly. The child looked at him calmly and seemed nonplussed by his words. "I know He can do anything. It doesn't make a bit of difference whether He heals me or not," she said calmly. "That's His business."[37]

The child's gracious acceptance of God's mysterious will poignantly brings to mind Flannery's words three months before she died from lupus. Writing to thank a friend for having had a Mass celebrated for her intentions, she commented, "I don't know what my intentions are, but I try to say that whatever suits the Lord suits me."[38]

Flannery never mentioned her struggle with lupus in the introduction to the sisters' book, but she did describe Mary Ann as facing "passive diminishments." This was a term, coined by the Jesuit priest Pierre Teilhard de Chardin, that Flannery applied to her own life in some of her letters, indicating a surrender to God's will and the acceptance of suffering. It included submitting to the slow process of dying that many people endure. Flannery struck another chord between herself and Mary Ann when she wrote in the introduction, "The creative action of the Christian's life is to prepare his death in Christ."[39] Toward the end, Mary Ann knew that death was near, and in her own little girl fashion, she readied herself to meet it. The woman writing the introduction also was, in her own way, preparing herself spiritually for death, which was just a few years away.

A Miniature Dominican

On Christmas Eve of 1960, Flannery announced the good news to Hester. The Catholic magazine *Jubilee* was going to publish her introduction, and the sisters were "tickled pink."[40] Flannery herself was a bit perturbed that *Jubilee* planned to use drawings of Mary Ann instead of photographs, since much time had been spent finding photographs: "Don't know what has made them change their minds—and all our fuss over getting the pictures."[41] Although Flannery does not say so in the letters, it is highly likely that the editors were apprehensive about publishing photos of the very deformed little girl, preferring to soften their shocking impact by using an artist's renderings instead.

More good news followed early in the New Year, when the book found a publisher (Farrar, Straus, and Cudahy). Writing to Giroux on January 23, 1961, Flannery described the sisters as "dancing jigs up & down the hall." She also mentioned that she had bet the sisters that no one would publish the book, which meant she was now "out a pair of peafowl."[42] Before the bishop would give his seal of approval, however, he requested two changes in the book. One scene had to go: the one where Mary Ann went to confession and the nuns overheard her saying "fifty times, Monsignor" to her confessor. After all, the confessional was supposed to be a private place. Flannery acquiesced, noting to Giroux, "Bishops will be Bishops."[43]

The other change involved the reinstatement of a memorable scene. It seems the little girl had wanted to be a sister, and shortly before her death the nuns had allowed her to become a tertiary, a member of the Third Order of Saint Dominic. In doing this the sisters had broken the rule that required tertiaries to be at least fifteen.[44] After the little girl got her wish, she chose the name Sister M. Loretta Dorothy and donned a miniature Dominican habit, in which she was later buried.[45] The sisters had worried about including these details in the book, until the bishop assured them they had done nothing wrong.

"I Am Sparing You"

Flannery poured plenty of energy into the entire manuscript, but she received credit only for writing the introduction, which was, no doubt, all she wanted. In truth, though, heavy editing sometimes involves re-writing, and the roles of editor and writer can become blurred, which seems highly likely with this project. Although she complained about the quality of the material that the nuns had sent her, the finished project is poignant, lively, and inspirational, just like the child herself.

As the book moved toward publication, there were some last-minute changes that surely had Flannery gnashing her teeth. When she had the manuscript ready to pop into the mail, the sisters suddenly decided to add a "few other little things." Flannery inserted two of the three incidents they sent her, but she dispensed with the third, which concerned Mary Ann's eating some applesauce. "I am sparing you," she told Giroux on December 8, 1960.[46]

After her initial work was done, Flannery also graciously offered to proofread the galleys, an onerous task. In April of 1961, the sisters visited Andalusia and delivered their copy of the proofs to her. When she later wrote to Sister Evangelist, she mentioned sending the sisters home that day with four baby geese for the children at the "Our Lady of Perpetual Help Free Cancer Home and Zoo."[47]

The sisters came up with some dramatic titles. There were, for example, *Song Without End* and *The Bridegroom Cometh*, both of which Flannery nixed. Instead, she suggested the simple *A Memoir of Mary Ann,* which they accepted reluctantly, judging it "very flat." Even after the manuscript was at the publisher's, the sisters still were coming up with titles and continuing to "issue bulletins" about changes.[48] In the end, the book bore the title that Flannery had suggested and was dedicated, at her request, to the memory of Nathaniel Hawthorne.

"A Genuine Miracle"

Despite her initial misgivings, Flannery finally admitted to seeing God's hand in the project. "I told the Sisters that if the child was a saint, her first miracle would be getting a publisher for the book," she wrote

Hester on February 4, 1961. "The more I think about the way that book was written, the more convinced I am that it is a genuine miracle."[49] The miraculous events, however, didn't end with finding a publisher. When the book came out, critics called it "heartwarming," "superb," and "triumphant."[50] And on July 22 of that year, Flannery announced to Hester that the book had been purchased by Burns and Oates of London, and would bear the title *The Death of a Child*. She added, "It is almost comical how speedily it is proceeding, this project of the Lord's."[51]

There was more good news. On September 24, Flannery wrote to Sister Josephine at the cancer home to enclose a copy of the "first pre-publication review" that Giroux had sent her. She called the positive review a "worthy send-off," because it had appeared in *The Kirkus Bulletin,* used by bookstore owners to decide which books to stock. "Mary Ann leaves no details unattended to," she added. She also asked Sister Josephine to share the review with Sister Evangelist.[52]

A few months later, Flannery wrote to Sister Evangelist to express her delight with the book's appearance. "Mary Ann doesn't owe me a thing but I wish you would ask her to help a friend of mine who has left the Church," she added.[53] Sister believed that Mary Ann was a saint, and apparently had told Flannery that the child would be showering blessings on her from heaven. Although she didn't mention a name, it is likely that Flannery had Hester in mind, since she had recently left the Church.

Long-lasting Consequences of Charity

Flannery's desire to help the sisters had far-reaching implications. On the most basic monetary level, the royalties helped the sisters in their ministry, which was entirely dependent on charitable contributions. The book also prompted readers to send the sisters letters and donations. Further, *Good Housekeeping* featured the story in its 1961 Christmas issue, paying $4,500 – a huge sum at the time – with $3,375 going to the sisters and $1,125 to Flannery.[54] The book also was snapped up by the Catholic Digest Book Club.[55]

There were also intangible effects of Flannery's generosity. Numerous letters mention the joy the sisters got from the project's success – they were "having a big bang at being authors." The sisters also became Flannery's dear friends, writing to her, praying for her, and visiting her over the years. At one point, they expressed their gratitude by presenting her with a small television, which they personally delivered when they visited Andalusia to pick up the peafowls they had won in the bet. Shortly thereafter, Flannery told a friend, "Me and ma have entered the twentieth century at last."[56]

✠   ✠   ✠   ✠

Mary Ann Long brought great joy into the lives of the sisters and the other patients at the cancer home. Her brief life would've had value even had no book been written about her, but because of the sisters' love for her and Flannery's willingness to help them, a lasting testimony about finding value in suffering and seemingly senseless pain, came into being. Mary Ann's life stands as a passionate witness to two Catholic beliefs that Flannery cherished: all human life is precious in God's eyes, and love always triumphs over suffering.

Flannery must have known how important the introduction to this book was, and how vividly it illuminated her own enduring faith in Christ – which persisted despite her agonizing physical decline. As we saw earlier, she perceived a mystical connection between Nathaniel Hawthorne, his daughter, and the little girl that the sisters cared for, but there obviously is another factor in this spiritual equation, and that is Flannery herself. Her words in the introduction conveyed to future readers, other members of the Communion of Saints, compelling insights about the ways the Catholic faith approaches the mystery of suffering.

In a letter to Hester on June 10, 1961, Flannery tied in her reflections on Mary Ann's suffering with her fiction, particularly *Wise Blood*, a book whose Christian overtones many readers missed. In the book Hazel Motes becomes a street-corner preacher of nihilism, denouncing Jesus at every opportunity. In the last few pages, Motes has a complete change of heart, becoming a martyr of sorts, wearing broken glass in his shoes and even blinding himself as a way to repent for his past sins.

In her letter, Flannery flatly rejected Hester's suggestion that she write an introduction to the second edition of *Wise Blood* to point out its religious significance to readers. All readers needed to know, Flannery insisted, was that she had written the novel from the standpoint of "orthodox Christianity." Although she does not elucidate, her clear meaning is that for an orthodox Christian, pain and distress – even that as extreme and horrific as Motes's – can be salvific. This, of course, was the main point of her introduction to the sisters' book. As Flannery stated, "In the future, anybody who writes anything about me is going to have to read everything I have written in order to make legitimate criticism, even and particularly the Mary Ann piece."[57]

CHAPTER 6

Tempering the Wind to the Lamb: Mentoring Other Writers

*W*riting fiction was Flannery's vocation, a word that comes from the Latin vocare, to call, and is often used in context of the priesthood or religious life. Indeed, Flannery's writing did share some features in common with religious life, since her work demanded a strict routine, many sacrifices, and long stretches of silence. "There is a great deal that has to either be given up or be taken away from you if you are going to succeed in writing a body of work," she told Hester.[1]

As she lived out her vocation, Flannery's faith provided the landmarks for the fictional universe she created. That universe included the Fall, the Incarnation, the Redemption, the Resurrection, and the operation of grace. "I feel... that being a Catholic has saved me a couple thousand years in learning to write," she noted.[2] Many letters reveal that her faith also prompted her to make the necessary sacrifices of time and energy to help other writers.

God's Business

Flannery believed that writing was a God-given talent. In an essay called "The Fiction Writer and His Country," she observed that "The Christian writer particularly will feel that whatever his initial gift is, it comes from God."[3] She also acknowledged that there was a mysterious element to this gift. As she penned her stories, she often felt like an artist facing an empty canvas with little idea of what images might start taking shape there.

She emphasized this mysterious nature of writing to Hester in 1956: "I certainly have no idea how I have written about some of the things I have, as they are things I am not conscious of having thought about one way or the other."[4] As for what might happen to her books once she had completed them, she believed that a writer should be resigned to God's will. Thus, she noted to the book editor at the Catholic newspaper that same year, "When the book leaves your hands, it belongs to God. He may use it to save a few souls or to try a few others, but I think that for the writer to worry about this is to take over God's business."[5]

"I Wish I Had Voices"

Although she recognized the mysterious nature of writing, Flannery wasn't keen on mystical descriptions of the nuts-and-bolts process. Once, her playwright friend Maryat Lee apparently mentioned that she had been hearing voices that inspired her. This prompted Flannery to reply in her self-deprecating fashion: "I wish I had Voices...or anyway distinct voices. I have something that might be a continuing muttering snarl like cats courting under the house, but no clear Voice in years."[6]

Voices or no voices, Flannery's fiction definitely annoyed some readers who complained that her characters were unpleasant and her plots shocking. To such criticism, her reply was short and sweet: "One writes what one can," she told Cecil Dawkins. She rather calmly accepted the fact that, for some mysterious reason, her particular God-given talent was describing misfits. This was not something to ponder or justify, it just was. "Vocation implies limitation but few people realize it who don't actually practice an art."[7]

Revolting Ruffled Curtains

Flannery took her vocation – her art – very seriously. She maintained a fixed writing schedule, and even when she was seriously ill, her chief concern was completing her stories. To avoid being distracted by the antics of the various birds that prowled around Andalusia, she kept her back to the window while she wrote. The setting for her creative work was definitely low-key. The abbess could not abide fancy touches in her room, and had no use for expensive furniture or elegant flourishes. Instead, she wrote each day on a "large ugly brown desk" with a manual typewriter sitting in a depression in the middle of it. In front of the desk was an orange crate, covered with mahogany stain and with the bottom knocked out. She used a cartridge-shell box to hold her papers. "All my paraphernalia is somewhere around this vital center," she said, "and a little rooting produces it."[8] When her "parent," as she often referred to Regina, tried to lend a decorative touch to her cell by installing "revolting ruffled curtains," Flannery demanded that they be removed, "lest they ruin my prose."[9] In her humble surroundings, she wrote fiction for about two hours in the mornings with letters written later in the day.

Dead or Alive

In many ways, Flannery's writing habits also mirrored her belief in the Communion of Saints. Although she wrote her drafts in solitude, she then shipped them out to friends and mentors for their comments, and invited their stories in return. For example, once Flannery had completed a draft of *The Violent Bear It Away,* which she had worked on for seven years, she didn't just send it off to a publisher, but instead relied on input from her community of writers. These included Caroline Gordon Tate, the Fitzgeralds, Hester, and others. Flannery's letters often show her expressing gratitude for her friends' suggestions, and then passing on the favor to other writers by the careful attention she gave to their manuscripts.

As a mentor to a community of fledgling authors, Flannery was firm but compassionate. In a letter to Hester on November 29, 1956, she described the ideal writing teacher as a midwife: "After you help deliver the *enfant*, it is ungracious to say, Madame, your child has two heads and will never grow up." Her way of teaching, she explained, was merely to announce if the story was dead or alive.[10] In her mentoring, Flannery modeled Christ's admonition to love our neighbors as ourselves. She admitted to Hester that she was not a very severe teacher because she recalled her own early days as a writer, when harsh advice might have caused her to give up. She was thus well aware that a teacher's comments could have devastating effects on students: "What is on the other side of the story is flesh and blood and you temper the wind to the lamb."[11]

There were limits, however, to what a mentor could do. Although a good teacher should consider the effects of criticism on a student, he also must consider the student's actual talent or lack thereof. When it came to writing fiction, a writer must fashion a world, characters, and a story. This ability to create life with words, Flannery said, "is essentially a gift." Clearly, someone who has the gift can develop it, but what about the person who lacks talent but still wants to write? That poor soul, she said, "might as well forget it."[12]

"Spiritually Empty" Stories

Critics and reviewers often dished out harsh comments about her own work, but Flannery didn't get discouraged. Instead, she put their stinging remarks to good use by sharing them with her friends. She wanted aspiring writers to know that others' opinions should not derail their efforts. Thus, in an early letter to Hester, she mentioned a review by a priest who had opined that Flannery's convictions might be Catholic, but her sensibility appeared to be Lutheran. She also mentioned another reviewer who called her stories "technically excellent; spiritually empty."[13]

Flannery did not mince words when it came to reviewers. Writing to author Ben Griffith, she told him about a review of *A Good Man Is Hard to Find* in *Time* magazine that nearly gave her "apoplexy" and another in *The Atlanta Journal* that "was so stupid it was painful." The latter review had been crafted by a lady who usually wrote about gardening, which prompted Flannery to remark, "They shouldn't have taken her away from the petunias."[14]

"Shaking and Speechless"

Unfortunately, even Flannery's own mother often missed the point of her daughter's stories. Flannery relates how one day Regina asked her why she didn't write something more popular, "instead of the kind of thing I do write." The situation is reminiscent of a heated confrontation between the aspiring, unpublished writer Asbury and his mother in "The Enduring Chill." The mother suggests that Asbury write a novel like *Gone with the Wind,* one that contains plenty of references to the Civil War. When he protests that he doesn't plan to write any such book, she changes her tactics, suggesting he write a poem instead. We can imagine sparks flying when Regina went on to ask Flannery: "Do you think... that you are really using the talent God gave you when you don't write something that a lot, a LOT, of people like?" Flannery confessed that her mother's criticism "always leaves me shaking and speechless, raises my blood pressure 140 degrees."[15]

Fortunately, many friends *did* recognize the point of Flannery's stories, and she valued their constructive appraisals. Accomplished writer Caroline Gordon Tate was high on the list. At one point, Flannery passed on to Hester one of her manuscripts bearing Tate's numerous comments and suggestions, as a way to show how much her own work depended on input from others. She confided, "I wouldn't let anybody see these but you."[16] Flannery added that she had learned more from working on that particular story than she had in a long time, "merely because [Caroline] has patience with me." Although Flannery humbly described herself as having a "few instincts," she said that her mentor had more, plus thirty more years of experience.[17]

Criticism from the Devil

Betty Hester was quite keen on getting her fiction published, and she sought Flannery's advice on numerous stories. At one point in early 1960, Hester had become quite depressed because someone had harshly criticized her manuscript, and she had written Flannery to complain. This letter prompted Flannery to try to bolster her friend's confidence with advice that should be posted on the bedroom wall of any aspiring writer: "Any criticism at all which depresses you to the extent that you feel you cannot ever write anything worth anything is from the Devil and to subject yourself to it is for you an occasion of sin." She added another strong note of encouragement: "In you, the talent is there, and you are expected to use it."[18]

Over the years, Flannery gave Hester plenty of excellent advice on improving her writing. "Experiment but for heaven sakes [avoid] writing exercises," she cautioned on December 11, 1956. As she gave advice to Hester, Flannery revealed the way her own stories took shape. For example, she said there was no need to have a plot in mind before sitting down to write: "Start simply with a character or anything that you can make come alive." This was how Flannery had written the story "Good Country People": she had begun one morning writing a description of two female acquaintances and decided to give one a wooden leg. Before long, she brought in the Bible salesman, but at first she didn't realize he would steal the wooden leg, and she herself was quite surprised when it happened. Flannery assured her friend that once she had a character, "he will create his own situation [which] will suggest some kind of resolution."[19]

Pushing a Stone Uphill

When Hester apologized for having sent her mentor a story that was clearly a flop, Flannery was quick to offer reassurance: "You must never apologize for sending me a story that don't [sic] work because that is the kind you learn on." To encourage Hester, Flannery admitted that she herself sometimes wrote for many months and then tore up everything. "My existence is full of stories that I had to put aside because I wasn't writing them the way they needed to be written."[20] Writing was indeed difficult for her, she admitted to Hester in the fall of that same year. Only the fictional characters Enoch Emery and Hulga had come easy: "The rest has been pushing a stone uphill with my nose."[21]

"You Sit There"

Another writer who sought Flannery's help was Cecil Dawkins, who evidently was struggling with establishing a fixed writing schedule, something that Flannery could definitely help her with, since she was such a creature of habit herself. As she put it in a letter to Dawkins on September 22, 1957, "I'm a full-time believer in writing habits, pedestrian as it all may sound." True, a genius might dispense with routine, but, "Most of us only have talent and this is simply something that has to be assisted all the time by physical and mental habits or it dries up and blows away."[22]

Alluding to her illness, Flannery explained to Dawkins how she had tailored her routine to her capabilities. She had energy only to write two hours a day, but she refused to let anything interfere with those two hours. She also told Dawkins that she always wrote at the same time and the same place. And even if she worked for months and had to throw everything away, she never believed that time was wasted.

Despite this excellent advice, Dawkins continued to struggle with establishing a routine. In a letter written a few years later, Flannery got to the heart of her friend's problem. "One reason you are not writing is that you are allowing yourself to read in the time set aside to write." She advised Dawkins to devote three hours each morning strictly to writing. This meant no reading, no talking, and no cooking: "No nothing, but you sit there."[23] A writer had to be ready to receive inspiration when it came.

"Cheers! $1000"

In her advice to Dawkins, Flannery hinted at the mystery that underpins the mundane act of sitting in front of a typewriter. "Something goes on that makes it easier when it does come well," she wrote. She added that "if you don't sit there every day, the day it would come well, you won't be sitting there."[24] Flannery also emphasized that a writer should find a solitary place to work, which meant that writing could be lonely at times. However, she wasn't about to call it a kind of martyrdom. After all, she had told Hester that she became nauseated when people mentioned the "loneliness of the artist."

Dawkins then evidently took seriously Flannery's advice about establishing a routine, because she eventually became quite a proficient writer. Flannery greatly admired Dawkins' stories, praising her for having a very good ear. At another time, Flannery said that it was "dangerous" to criticize Dawkins' stories because they were so good. A letter to Dawkins in 1959 opened: "Cheers, cheers! $1000," alluding to Dawkins' having received that quite-hefty sum for a story. "Now that they've taken one, they'll probably take another and you won't never have to go to work," Flannery wrote, adding humbly that she had never received that much money for her own fiction.[25]

Flannery continued working behind the scenes like a guardian angel to help her friend. On January 26, 1962, she wrote Dawkins a glowing letter of recommendation to attend Yaddo, the artists' colony. The words of praise worked, and Dawkins landed a spot there. Soon Flannery was reminiscing about her own stint at the colony years before, saying it all sounded "powerful familiar," even down to the presence of a studio squirrel.[26]

✠   ✠   ✠   ✠

Unfortunately, Hester never experienced the joy of having her stories accepted for publication, but she did at least see her name in print, thanks to Flannery having recommended her as a book reviewer for *The Bulletin.* Dawkins, on the other hand, went on to do her mentor proud. In a letter written in November of 1963, Flannery mentioned to another friend that three collections of Dawkins' stories had been reviewed in the *New York Times* Book Section.[27] Shortly after, Flannery told Dawkins that she had read a good review of her book *The Quiet Enemy* in the *London Times* Literary Supplement.[28] With her mentor's blessings, Dawkins eventually adapted several of Flannery's stories into a full-length play, *The Displaced Person,* which was produced in New York City in 1965. She also went on to publish a number of mysteries.

It's highly appropriate that Flannery's disease was named after the wolf, since it savagely stalks its victims, robbing them of mobility and energy. Because of her illness, Flannery's friends surely would have excused her if she had refused to look over their manuscripts by offering that age-old excuse writers are so familiar with: "I don't have time, I'm on a deadline." Instead, she gave lavishly of her time and talent by poring over their manuscripts and offering generous amounts of encouragement and advice that came directly from her own monastic approach to writing.

If writing truly is a calling from God, as she believed, then, like other callings, it demands sacrifices, and the writer who insists on wasting time is squandering something precious. Thus it is little surprise that a woman whose schedule was fixed, starting and ending each day with prayer and always including writing, would continue to remind her friends about the importance of routine. As the years went on, Flannery's stores of energy became even more diminished, yet even then she did not beg off when they sought her critiques.

In fact, her ministry as a mentor continued right until the end. Sessions recalled visiting her in the hospital two months before her death and noticing that near her bed were some theology books, plus "manuscripts from hopeful writers."[29]

CHAPTER 7

Mortification of the Mind: Writing for the "Cathlick" Press

Some of Flannery's writing projects brought her little pleasure, and topping the list were book reviews written for what she darkly called "the Cathlick paper." [1] It is true that she was paid for her efforts, but she put up with the annoyances for a nobler reason. Especially as her mobility became more curtailed by her illness, writing for the Catholic press was another ministry that she could perform without leaving her little room in Andalusia. That she suffered for this ministry seems clear. There were times when the editors garbled her words and sparred with her about the books she wanted to review.

She also suffered at the hands of Catholic reviewers, who, for the most part, didn't understand her fiction. At times they even declared that it wasn't Catholic, maybe because her stories largely featured Protestant characters and lacked an obvious Catholic message. There were, however, a few bright "Cathlick" souls who recognized the brilliance of her writing and understood the deeper, orthodox elements.

Corrupting Your Taste

On February 11, 1956, Flannery announced to Hester that she was working on a book review for *The Bulletin*, the diocesan newspaper. With her tongue firmly in cheek, she called the upcoming review her "emergence into the Catholic Press."[2] There are many acerbic comments about the Catholic press (the motto of which, she wrote, should be, "We guarantee to corrupt nothing but your taste."[3]) sprinkled throughout her letters, but she persevered with the reviews, critiquing about a dozen books a year.

Flannery wasn't shy about expressing her opinion on the quality of the material she was reviewing. For example, on February 19, 1956, she wrote to John Lynch, another Catholic writer, to tell him that she'd had the "doubtful honor" of reviewing *All Manner of Men*, a selection of twenty-five short stories by Catholic writers. Flannery thought the stories read as if they'd been authored by college students, and added that piety was indeed portrayed in them, "but not always at a depth that would make it acceptable," whereas sin was "conspicuous by its absence." Her major complaint centered on the overly pious plot lines: "All those baby stories and nun stories and young girl stories—a nice vapid Catholic distrust of finding God in action of any range and depth." She added that this was not the kind of Catholicism that had saved her so many years in learning how to become a writer, "but then this is not Catholicism at all."[4] About a week later, mentioning this same book review to Hester, she noted dryly that it was Lent and "we are advised to practice mortification."[5]

Literature Fit for Burning

Lynch had left teaching to work for *Ave Maria*, a Catholic publication, with which Flannery admitted she wasn't familiar. Still, based on her own experience with other publications, she didn't hesitate to criticize it. "This vapid Catholicism can't influence you except to want to be shut of it," she complained in that same letter to him. "The Catholic influence has to come at a deeper level." No doubt responding to a comment in Lynch's letter about having a family, she told him point-blank that she believed "you [would] do better to have a large family than any number of books." She went on to wonder if working for *Ave Maria* would be worse than teaching. Perhaps she was thinking about the times when she was invited to give talks, and how much energy that required. "I have never taught but I can imagine its being a terrible drain on your creative powers."[6]

Some of Flannery's complaints about writing for the diocesan newspaper are screamingly funny. Evidently *The Bulletin's* book review editor, Eileen Hall, managed to get on Flannery's nerves by failing to publish her reviews in a timely fashion. As Flannery lamented to Hester, the paper had "thousands of [my] reviews on stock... and she just don't print any of them."[7] Flannery also judged the overall quality of the newspaper's writing to be dismal. Sending the book page to Hester, she remarked that the rest of the issue was devoted to descriptions of St. Patrick's Day parades. Given her own dim view of this particular celebration, it is little wonder that she called the newspaper the kind of literature she "approved of burning."[8]

Her "Pious" Reaction

Then there was the matter of sloppy editing. Flannery complained bitterly when copy editors incorrectly changed the spelling of words in her reviews, for example turning "engender" into "endanger" and

"Gnostic" into "agnostic."[9] Some of the editorial changes were clearly made in error, but others appear to have been intentional. Once Flannery had noted in a lecture that many Catholics mistakenly believed that an author was writing exclusively for them. When an article about the talk was published, however, editors replaced the word "Catholics" with "Americans." As she told Hester, "They didn't want to hear what I said and when they heard it they didn't want to believe it and so they changed it." In that same speech, Flannery had shared her blunt opinion that "the average Catholic reader was a Militant Moron," but that quote, not too surprisingly, didn't show up in print.[10]

After she wrote for the Jesuit magazine *America*, the scathing remarks intensified. "I do not mind at all being corrected," she said, "but I think I should have been asked to make the correction myself."[11] The paragraph in question contained what was to Flannery an important distinction. She had written that "the responsibility for souls was the business of the Church and the responsibility of the artist was to his art." The magazine, however, quoted her as saying something very different: that the artist, as well as the Church, had a responsibility for souls.[12] Her self-described "pious reaction" to the situation, as shared with Hester, was "to hell with it, I have other things to do."[13]

Corporal Works of Mercy

Although she didn't believe writers had a responsibility to bring about their readers' salvation, Flannery did recognize the universal Christian obligation to perform corporal works of mercy: including feeding the hungry, visiting the sick, and clothing the naked. But over the years as her symptoms from lupus worsened – she was forced to begin using crutches in the fall of 1955 – her physical limitations meant that the "only corporal work of mercy open" to her, as she told Hester in April, 1957, was writing for Catholic newspaper and magazines.[14] And even if this service was just "a drop in the bucket," she felt it was the right thing to do.

Writing for Catholic publications was for her certainly a penitential practice, but she had another admirable motive. As Carter W. Martin notes in *The Presence of Grace*, a collection of Flannery's book reviews, she also wanted to help raise the level of Catholic intellectual life by writing for the ordinary layman, rather than for theologians and priests.[15] Thus, despite her bitter comments to friends and humorous jabs at editors, Martin says she regarded her book reviews as an obligation and "a serious part of her life in the Church."[16]

In her typical low-key manner, Flannery used humor to downplay her contributions. She wrote at one point to ask an editor, "Send me any scourgy book you like for my advent penance."[17] When Hester, who was also reviewing books, grew discouraged by the way Hall was treating her reviews, however, Flannery's tone became more serious. And in encouraging her friend, she revealed her deepest motivation for writing for the "Cathlick" press: "What you do for the *Bulletin* you do for God."[18]

Scandalizing the Little Ones

Sparks really flew when Flannery and the *Bulletin* editor, Eileen Hall, locked horns, as they did over one particular book Flannery wanted to review. The editor fretted about the plot, deeming the book as potentially scandalizing to the "little ones."[19] *The Malefactors,* written by Caroline Gordon, Flannery's beloved mentor, featured an unfaithful husband who undergoes a religious conversion. Although today the topic would be considered unremarkable, in 1956 the very mention of an adulterous marriage had the editor shaking in her boots.

Flannery was certainly familiar with the charge of shocking readers. Many people, including some of her relatives, reacted to her stories with that very complaint. When *Wise Blood* came out in 1952, reactions in Milledgeville were "grisly," according to Robert Fitzgerald. In fact, Regina worried so much about cousin Katie's reaction to the book that she wanted Flannery to write a special introduction to be pasted on the inside of the old lady's edition, which, said Flannery, was supposed to have been written in the tone of the *Sacred Heart Messenger.* Writing to Hall on March 10, 1956, four years after *Wise Blood*'s publication, Flannery said that she had, at first, worried about scandalizing people, since at one time she had fancied that what she wrote "was highly inflammatory."[20] Concerned, she had talked with a priest, and he had reassured her, "You don't have to write for fifteen-year-old girls." In an obvious jibe at Hall's readers, Flannery opined that many people are seventy-five years old but harbor a fifteen-year-old girl in their heads.[21]

Although the topic was reviewing Gordon's novel, the discussion with Hall reveals quite a bit about Flannery's own approach to writing fiction. To bolster her point of view, Flannery mentioned Francois Mauriac, the Nobel Prize winner who was considered one of the greatest Catholic writers of the twentieth century. Mauriac had been very troubled when one of his readers, a young boy, wrote him to say that he had contemplated suicide after reading one of Mauriac's novels. After reflection, Mauriac decided that he was not responsible for the boy's lack of maturity. His advice, she noted to Hall, was simple and solid: in his book *God and Mammon* he advised a novelist to "purify the source," which is, of course, the mind. Flannery emphasized that an author's intentions make a difference. If a book proceeds from a pure source, it's not the author's fault if it becomes distorted in the public eye. "When you write a novel," Flannery wrote, "if you have been honest about it and if your conscience is clear, then it seems to me that you have to leave the rest in God's hands."[22]

Writing about the Vulgar to Make Grace Believable

When Hall fretted about the matter of bad taste, Flannery had another ready answer. No doubt some people would also find Christ's association with Mary Magdalene to be in bad taste, she wrote. She explained that fiction is supposed to represent life. "If you're writing about the vulgar, you have to prove they're vulgar by showing them at it."[23] She did not believe, she went on to say, in vulgarity for its own sake; she had little use for authors who followed every character into the bedroom. But for her, truly worrisome offenses in fiction had to do with moral errors, "when right is held up as wrong, or wrong as right."

Flannery ended the letter by giving Hall the final say. "Don't feel you have to review the Gordon book if you think it would cause the *Bulletin* embarrassment or trouble." Nonetheless, although she promised that she would "certainly understand," she couldn't resist a final stinging remark: "Most of your readers wouldn't like *The Malefactors* if it were favorably reviewed by Pius XII."[24]

The editor finally surrendered, and on March 31, 1956 Flannery's review of *The Malefactors* appeared in the newspaper. In the plot summary, Flannery told readers that the protagonist had become involved with a "lady intellectual poet," and this relationship had taken him "away from his wife." But she also wrote about his returning to the wife, who had attempted suicide and who ultimately "found her way to the Church." Calling the book "profoundly Catholic in theme," Flannery said it was doubtful the work would receive the attention it deserved from Catholic readers because they were liable to be "shocked by the kind of life portrayed in it." She also suspected that secularists wouldn't appreciate the work either because they wouldn't accept the reality of supernatural grace in the plot. And in a comment that could apply to her frustration over the way her own stories were received, she added, "Making grace believable to the contemporary reader is the almost insurmountable problem of the novelist who writes from the standpoint of Christian orthodoxy."[25]

Nasty Little Stories

Much to her surprise, one of Flannery's books – *A Good Man Is Hard to Find* – received a favorable review in *The Bulletin*. She expressed great pleasure to Hester on March 10, 1956, because she had a "slew of old lady friends" who had been "waiting patiently these many years for me to get enough rope to hang myself with." Evidently the reviewer had mentioned a Catholic element in Flannery's writing, which led Flannery to remark triumphantly that those ladies "never supposed there was a Catholic influence... in the nasty little stories." She didn't think the review would change their opinions, but at least it would "give them pause."[26]

Other Catholic reviewers were far less kind. In a letter written two years later, Flannery asked Hester, "Did you read about how disgusting my works are in the *Commonweal* last week?" She added, "I ain't quite the darling of the Catholic press yet, huh?"[27] On March 14, 1959, she lamented about an article in *Catholic World* discussing the future of the Catholic novel. She noted that it had been written "by some academic dope at Loyola in New Orleans" who railed against Catholic writers whose works were "depressing." The author insisted Catholics should write instead about liturgical movements "and the Catholic attitude to race relations."[28]

All Our Heads May Roll

Flannery's struggles with the diocesan newspaper went on for years. In October of 1956, she remarked to Hester, who was also doing reviews for the paper, that it was high time Hall gave up the book page. One of her complaints was that a girl named Wenonah Chambers was reviewing books with gushing comments like, "All boys and girls will love this book." Yet Flannery had to put up with Hall for another four years, however, before Hall moved on. When Leo J. Zuber, an Atlanta resident, took over the book page, Flannery at first had her doubts: "A man probably won't have the time or patience to fool with it long, but we shall see."[29]

Her misgivings about Zuber proved unfounded, however. The two got along famously, and the entire Zuber family would often visit Andalusia. When word got around that *The Bulletin* was slated to get a new managing editor, she expressed hope that Zuber would continue overseeing book reviews. Aware that a new boss might clear the decks entirely, in the fall of 1962 she worried,

"All our heads may roll."[30] As the New Year opened in 1963, Flannery's thoughts about the new managing editor were rather grim, since he had eliminated the book page entirely, at least for a while.[31]

Champion of the Holy

Although she was not the darling of many Catholic reviewers, there were some priests who warmly praised Flannery's fiction and recognized it as deeply Catholic. One was Father Edward J. Romagosa, a Jesuit who was teaching English literature and Biblical Greek to the scholastics in Juniorate in Grand Coteau, Louisiana. In the spring of 1959, he wrote Flannery to tell her that his students were reading her short story "The River," which he described as exemplifying the power of faith in ordinary life.

She was probably relieved that the priest saw this as the underlying theme in the story, for many readers might miss that point due to the story's shocking ending. In "The River," a young boy – the son of parents who spend their evenings drinking heavily and who think religion is a big joke – is taken for the day to the home of a babysitter, Mrs. Connin. She is a down-home country woman who shows the child more tenderness than he ever gets from his parents. Shocked to discover that the boy has never heard of Jesus, she sets things straight, giving him a few Bible lessons. She also takes the little fellow to the river, where a preacher baptizes him, telling him something that the child surely never heard from his own parents: "You count now."

The experience makes such a deep impression on this neglected child that he returns to the river on his own, determined to baptize himself and find the "Kingdom of Christ." Although he doesn't realize it, the child is being pursued by Mr. Paradise, one of Flannery's most diabolical figures. When the child notices that Mr. Paradise – who looks like a giant pig and who brandishes a large peppermint stick – is after him, he plunges beneath the water and is caught by the swiftly moving current. Although he is drowning, it is in the river that finally all his "fury and fear" leave him. His faith has saved him from a terrible fate in a lecher's grip.

In her reply to Father Romagosa, dated May 4, 1959, Flannery mentioned that she was writing *The Violent Bear It Away,* which was about a boy who was "trying to escape the Lord's call to be a prophet." Describing herself as "waiting to see if this is going to be called a Catholic novel by my brethren," she expressed her appreciation to the priest for his interest.[32] In her next letter, written in January of 1960, she mentioned her suspicion that the novel would be "heartily trounced by one and all."[33]

Father Romagosa had high praises for Flannery when two years later he introduced her to an audience at the University of Southwestern Louisiana. He described her as a defender of the Catholic faith who "championed the sacred and the holy by exposing its enemies: proud and complacent rationalism that refuses to bend the mind before the revealing word: self-pitying tenderness that turns every pain into an argument against the existence of God."[34]

"My Eyes Are Scorched"

Father Youree Watson was another Jesuit who waxed enthusiastic about Flannery's talents. They met in 1957 for the first time, when Father Watson was teaching philosophy to Jesuit seminarians at Spring Hill College in Mobile, Alabama, and they began writing each other that year. In the preface to their correspondence, published in 1979, he remembered her in glowing terms as "intelligent and well-read, yet not talkative, much less self-assertive." Praising her opinions as modest and sincere, he described her as "beautifully and quite deliberately simple."[35]

Very few letters that Flannery received from her many correspondents are still in existence today, but the small cache from Father Watson is a notable exception. Writing to her on July 31, 1958, Father Watson praised her story "The Enduring Chill," while also lauding "A View of the Woods," which he called "extraordinarily gripping."[36] She later sent him a copy of *The Violent Bear It Away*, telling him that she feared its reception was "going to be very poor – the grotesque infuriates everybody."[37]

It turns out she was quite right; one critic, R.O. Bowen, decided that the book was distinctly "anti-Catholic" and described it as "a pointless bit of comic book sentimentality." Father Watson, however, wrote back a very long letter, filled with strong encouragement. To him, her novel was a powerful book, comparable to *The Brothers Karamazov*. He praised her wit, her use of dialogue, and the poetry of her language. She must have been thrilled when he recognized Satan as the stranger that dominates Tarwater's consciousness and delighted when he described the story as demonstrating that "religion is right, irreligion wrong."[38] He also recognized the bread of life, for which Tarwater hungered, as a symbol of the Eucharist, which gives life its supreme meaning. "My eyes are scorched," he wrote, thanking her for the gift of writing the book.

✠ ✠ ✠ ✠

It wasn't just the professional fiction critics who misunderstood Flannery's work. As we have noted, her own mother often misunderstood her stories and thought she was wasting her talent. Old ladies in her town often were horrified by her plots, which featured prostitutes, drunkards, killers, and shocking moments such as self-mutilation ("Wise Blood"), child suicide ("The Lame Shall Enter First"), and seduction ("Good Country People"). If public acclaim was limited, so were the financial rewards, as she candidly admitted to writer John Lynch: "There's no money in it and little consolation except that it looks good when you have to fill out a form... And a year later you will get a few letters from your friends saying they saw your book for 33 cents on a remainder table." She added plaintively: "At least this is what is always happening to me."[39]

Flannery continued to write her fiction, however, because it was the one thing she felt she could do well, the one talent that she clearly could see coming from God. She also believed that writing fiction was her way to glorify God in return. Following the principles of St. Thomas Aquinas, she held that a good work of fiction doesn't exist to reform or convert someone, but is rather "a good in and by itself." A story or novel needn't have any utilitarian value at all, because "what is good in itself glorifies God because it reflects God."[40]

Along this line of thinking, it's clear that other aspects of her writing, whether it was corresponding with friends or writing for Catholic publications, also proceeded from her belief that she was heeding God's calling, and that this was a good thing to do, in and of itself. Thus, even when she wrote reviews that the editor failed to publish, gave friends tips on stories that never saw the light of day, or wrote for an audience whose maturity she suspected to match the level of teen-agers, she persevered, because it was all part of her vocation: the reason God made her.

IV

Conversion of Heart

The child knelt down between her mother and the nun and they were well into the "Tantum Ergo" before her ugly thoughts stopped and she began to realize that she was in the presence of God.

—*"A Temple of the Holy Ghost"*

CHAPTER 8

Genius and Much Grace: The Priests in Flannery's Life

"*All good Catholics become anti-clerical sooner or later. It is a noble and honorable tradition.*"[1] *Coming from a faithful and obedient Catholic like Flannery, these words are definitely shocking, and we might be tempted to discount them as an offhand comment. Yet it was not an isolated remark: in another letter, for example, she described a visitor as "properly anti-clerical."[2] Was Flannery herself anti-clerical? As we shall see, it's true that some of her letters contain sharp jabs at bishops and priests whose behavior she judged as falling short of the mark.*

However, the letters make it quite clear that her remarks were not intended to harm the Church. Rather she meant to emphasize a critical truth: it is a fallen world, and this means that all human beings, including the clergy, are capable of sin. And yet, "The Church's nature is to survive all crises—in however battered a fashion."[3]

The Bishop's Fund-Raising Ads

In her letters Flannery delighted in describing the ridiculous and often annoying traits of other people. So while she might be accused of being "anti-clerical" in that she certainly didn't spare priests the barbs of her wit, she might also then be dubbed anti-Irish, since she enthusiastically poked fun at members of her own ethnic group. As we've seen, she was quite critical of the local pastor at Sacred Heart Church, calling him "his reverence" – largely because he had a rigid personality and went so far overboard in celebrating St. Patrick's Day. It's little wonder that when another priest recommended that she read a book about the Irish people, she delivered a dead-pan response: "I get enough of them from the pulpit."

At other times, Flannery expressed annoyance about one particular clergyman's overemphasis on fund-raising, which she found inappropriate for a man of the cloth. "The Bishop ought to get himself to Atlanta and confirm the people that want confirming," she wrote to Hester on May 19, 1956. "That is one thing the bishop is good for besides collecting funds." In that same letter, she dug the knife in a bit deeper when she mentioned that the *Bulletin's* book editor was not printing many reviews, an oversight she attributed to lack of room in the paper due to the bishop's "bloody ads for his campaign."[4]

Dominican Salt Mines

Flannery did have great respect for one well-known clergyman, Monsignor Romano Guardini, who had authored one of her favorite books *The Lord.* Writing to Hester early in 1956, she praised Guardini as free of smugness, a sin to which she believed many clergy fell prey when they became published authors – and which she had noticed in herself.[5]

In contrast, she was harshly critical of another clergyman-author, Cardinal Francis Joseph Spellman, whom she called "Frank the Spell man" and whose "poorly written" book *The Foundling* she thought would make a good door stop.[6]

Writing to the Fitzgeralds, she quipped that the "lay committee to advise Cardinal Spellman on how to keep his feet out of his mouth should certainly reorganize." It seems that Spellman had publicly condemned the movie *Baby Doll*, and although Flannery herself thought it a "dirty little piece of trash," she thought his reasons for condemning it weren't strong enough.[7] In another letter, this time to Hester, she mentioned that Mauriac had written about sitting next to Cardinal Spellman at some function and later said that he would have felt more "spiritual kinship" with the Dalai Lama.[8]

Other clergy grieved her when they made public pronouncements that, she thought, only revealed their ignorance. For example, in fall of 1957, she complained to Hester about "Father H.," saying he should be spent for a "reflective spell" to the nearest "Dominican salt mine." This priest had incurred Flannery's wrath by claiming publicly that Maritain had no influence over Catholic students at Princeton, a comment that she felt reflected badly on the students. She said that Father H. was the kind of priest that needed prayer, and added that she had reminded herself of this but failed to do it.[9]

The First Needle in the Haystack

Flannery might have quipped that anti-clericalism was a "noble" tradition, and she wasn't hesitant to criticize clergymen in her letters, but we know that she corresponded with two priests, Fathers Watson and

Romagosa, whose opinions she clearly respected. She had met them through another Jesuit friend who over the years had prayed for Flannery, visited her, and comforted her. He was James Hart McCown, who was born in Mobile, Alabama, in 1911 and was affectionately known as "Hooty." As he remarked in a poignant reminiscence written about fifteen years after her death, Father McCown served as a spiritual adviser to Flannery, who confided in him and sought his input on theological matters.[10]

Father McCown was also a great fan of Flannery's fiction. Before their first meeting at Andalusia, he had written her a letter, enclosing some books and magazines that he thought she would like. In her first letter to him, dated January 19, 1956, she thanked him and enclosed her novel *Wise Blood,* asking his opinion of it.[11] Its theme, she explained, was the loss of faith, although she had not used an explicitly Catholic background in the book. About a month later, Flannery reported that Father McCown made a rather dramatic appearance at Andalusia, showing up unannounced in a white Cadillac "to tell me that he had read and liked my stories." His positive reaction to the stories in *A Good Man Is Hard to Find* stunned her: "No priest has ever said turkey-dog to me about liking anything I wrote."[12] As she later remarked to Father Romagosa, even though she thought modern fiction should be part of a priest's training, she had met few priests interested in fiction. Father McCown was to her the "first needle in the haystack."[13]

A black-and-white Cadillac brought her new friend to Andalusia on his second visit, inspiring great curiosity in Flannery, who couldn't resist asking him about the cars. She discovered they were owned by a fellow whom Father McCown was bringing into the Church, and that day she sent the car owner home with a copy of *Wise Blood,* since he had admitted to having a hankering for novels with "a good many trashy spots." She told Hester, "I am waiting for his comment on *Wise Blood.*"[14]

The Priest and the Whiskey Salesman

In his reminiscence about Flannery, Father McCown gave his own colorful version of their first meeting. He had expected to meet a "smart-looking, independent-acting lady author," but the young woman at Andalusia certainly did not match the image. She had sharp blue eyes and a roundish face, puffed and a bit blotchy from the medication she was taking for lupus. Wearing old jeans and a brown blouse, and leaning on aluminum crutches, Flannery had opened the door and greeted him and his friend with a simple "Howdy." When he'd mentioned that he had liked her stories very much, she beamed a big smile. "Proud you did. Wanna come in?"[15] Father McCown and Flannery went on to have a lively discussion that day, and he was so impressed that he alerted Father Harold Gardiner, the literary editor at *America.*[16] Before long, Gardiner contacted the "lady author" and asked her to write a column for the magazine.[17]

Father McCown also set the record straight about the varicolored Cadillacs. It seems he was the assistant pastor at St. Joseph Catholic Church in Macon at the time, and he didn't own a car. Getting to Milledgeville, forty miles away, presented a problem that he solved by begging a ride with a man he described candidly as a "fat, big-hearted...whiskey salesman." This man happened to love new Cadillacs. "So, when you read [in *The Habit of Being*] about me coming to her house first in a white Cadillac, then in a black one, please do not misinterpret me," he pleaded. A self-described "red-hot, zealous, young" priest, Father McCown would beg many rides to visit his new friend at Andalusia. As they sat on the porch talking, the indomitable Regina often placed herself at the "dead center" of their every conversation, steering discussions to topics like the Communion fast, nuns' habits, and his opinion of priests running around in gray suits.[18]

Over the years, Father McCown came to treasure his Milledgeville friend's "short, salty judgments."[19] On one of his visits, McCown suggested that Flannery might do a bit of Catholic polemical writing. As he stated in his reminiscence, he felt that she could be "using that well-honed intellect to defend Holy Church against her enemies, especially the Georgia Baptists." She would have none of it, however. "That ain't my dish of tea," she replied tartly. Recalling the interchange, McCown admitted that this particular salty judgment of Flannery's had taught him "a lesson about integrity in art."[20]

In Mobile Every Weekend

The young Jesuit shared his writer friend's deadpan sense of humor, and her disdain for Catholic literary critics. Writing to the Fitzgeralds on January 22, 1956, Flannery mentioned having told Father McCown about a nun in Minneapolis who wrote good poetry. He had immediately quipped: "Boy, I bet she's crucified."[21] In December of that year, Flannery told Hester about some literary advice he had given her. She had been worried that the editor of *America* might condense one of her articles rather than letting her shorten it herself. She wrote the editor to express her concern, and then asked Father McCown if perhaps she'd hurt the man's feelings. He minced no words in his reply: "You ought to just tell him to keep his dirty red pencil off your manuscript."[22]

It's also clear from the correspondence that Father McCown didn't mind being kidded. In a letter dated January 12, 1958, Flannery told him that some of her friends had met a Father Murray from Spring Hill, Alabama. "They asked him about you, feeling very sorry for you stuck off in that retreat house," she noted. But it seems Father Murray didn't think Father McCown was suffering too terribly, for he also remarked, "Oh, we see him in Mobile every weekend." We can imagine Flannery chuckling as she delivered the punch line to Father McCown: "They like to have killed themselves laughing."[23]

"You Have Relieved a Lot of Pain"

Over the years that followed, Flannery wrote about sixty letters to her Jesuit friend and spiritual director. He could see that she had a vast knowledge of Catholic theology, but she still sought his guidance when she ran into trouble with the everyday practice of her faith. He never divulged her personal spiritual problems, but after her death, he described her as someone in whom sophistication co-existed with a "delicacy of conscience."[24] Although he gave no examples, we can surmise that, despite her sharp wit and her stories' incisive observations about human behavior, she tended to anguish over small transgressions in her life, and turned to Father McCown, her confessor, to help her sort out true sins from imagined ones.

It is apparent that Flannery considered Father McCown a good spiritual director and confessor. This was for her a rare find, since as she had earlier told another correspondent, directing others requires "a kind of genius and much grace." In a letter written on

Groundhog Day, 1958, Flannery promised to follow the Jesuit's spiritual advice, although she didn't specify what it was. "It relieves my mind of a burden that was keeping me off and on from doing my work. When you can't resolve these things it is a great relief to be told what to do."[25] About four years later, she wrote simply, "Cheers and many thanks again. You have relieved a lot of pain."[26]

In another letter, she asked Father McCown to set the record straight on something a nun had told one of her friends, namely that "anyone who hadn't heard of Jesus would be damned."[27] Flannery wanted to be absolutely sure that the Church didn't teach such a thing. Although we don't have Father McCown's letter to her, we can assume that he assured her that she was correct.

Writing on another Groundhog Day, Flannery asked for Father McCown's prayers as she headed to Chicago, where she would deliver a talk to the "city interleckchuls."[28] Given her apprehension about giving talks, her need for prayers was understandable. In a letter to a friend two months later, she recounted a particularly uncomfortable moment when she was helping with writing classes at the University of Chicago. The students had quickly run out of things to ask her, and one afternoon, after a ten-minute silence, a girl had asked, "Miss O'Connor, what are the Christmas customs in Georgia?"[29]

"SOS Spiritual Advice"

One particularly thorny theological problem that Father McCown helped Flannery solve arose in 1957. It seems the minister of the Episcopal church in Milledgeville had come to her with a request: he wanted to launch a discussion group on the topic of theology in modern literature, and hoped she would host it. She agreed, and soon the group was gathering on Monday nights at Andalusia. The assembly consisted of one Catholic (Flannery), a couple of Presbyterians, and a few Episcopalians. (The latter was a denomination she couldn't resist poking fun at. "Scratch an Episcopalian and you're liable to find most anything," she quipped to Father McCown on December 29, 1957.) She wrote the letter because she was having problems with the group and needed his "expert SOS spiritual advice."[30]

As she told Father McCown, as the only Catholic in the group she felt she was representing "the Holy Roman Catholic & Apostolic Church." Clearly, she wanted to make a good impression. The problem was that the minister wanted the group to read a book by André Gide, but it was considered sinful for Catholics to read this book, since it was on the "Index," a list of forbidden books. Flannery confided to her spiritual director that she didn't want to ask her parish priest for help with this matter. After all, the man had denied permission to some local women, "pillars of the church," who wanted to read Jehovah Witness pamphlets. "He is a letter of the law man, no ifs, ands, or buts, and very hard to approach anyway."

Obviously, she could have ignored the ban, but she did not take the precepts of the Church lightly. She confided to Father McCown that she despised Gide, but she still wanted to take part in the discussion, so she asked his permission to read the book in question. Aware that Protestants sometimes had difficulty understanding Catholic rules, she added, "All these Protestants will be shocked if I say I can't get permission to read Gide."[31]

Humility and Obedience

Today, many people might be puzzled to learn that a brilliant writer like Flannery felt she needed to ask a priest for permission to read a book. This seems like a small matter, but it beautifully illuminates her devotion to her faith. She recognized the Church as an authority higher than her own individual personality because she believed that the Church's teachings on faith and morals were directed by Christ. This fact may be hard to fathom for secularists, who can't conceive of an artist being guided by anything higher than individual conscience. However, as Father McCown described her, Flannery O'Connor was a woman who "drew her strength and vision from her Church's firm guidelines."

Especially today, when so-called "cafeteria Catholics" pick and choose among Church teachings, Flannery stands out as a shining role model: she was humble enough to ask permission and obedient enough to forgo reading the book if the answer was "no." This same obedience shone forth in a 1962 letter to Leo Zuber, then the book review editor of *The Bulletin*. She already had reviewed books by the mystical theologian Pierre Teilhard de Chardin, and she said she was interested in critiquing another one, but because the Vatican had issued a warning about de Chardin's writings, she suggested to Zuber that a "clerical gentleman" review the book instead.[32]

This little exchange tells us quite a bit about Flannery's real respect for the clergy. A bonafide anti-clericalist would show little concern for a Vatican-issued warning about a particular writer. In fact, had Flannery been truly anti-clerical, she might have been very eager to review the book as a protest against the Church's hierarchy. Lest we portray her as an overly respectful daughter of the Church, however, it's also worth mentioning that

Flannery also outspokenly wished the Church had offered not only a list of forbidden books, but required ones also.

Spirit of the Law

Father McCown came to Flannery's rescue by giving her a dispensation to read the forbidden book in her theology group. As he wrote years later, he believed that every Catholic has an obligation to obey Church law, but "an even higher obligation to protect the Church from ridicule."[33] She wrote to thank him on January 12, 1958, saying that she would use the *epeikia* – a breaking of the letter of the law in order to preserve the spirit – "and also invoke that word, which is very fancy."

Ironically, the whole issue about the forbidden book became moot, based on simple economics: Gide's book cost thirty-five cents, which the group considered too expensive. Father McCown's efforts were not in vain, however, since the group was also expressing interest in a book by Jean-Paul Sartre, another author with works on the Index. "If you can include him in with Gide, I'd be obliged," she added in that same letter.[34]

The theology meetings became increasingly burdensome for Flannery. In her opinion, the group members were trying so hard to be polite that few really important topics could be plumbed. She also noted darkly to Father McCown that "Nobody knows anything about theology." And in her inimitable fashion, she complained to Hester that the main result of their discussions was that the "damn room" had to be aired out afterwards to remove the stench of cigarettes.[35]

Measuring Sins with a Slide Rule

In Flannery's day, eating fish on Friday was practically synonymous with being Catholic. She did not live to see the day when the no-meat rule became optional, but if she had, she probably would have continued that penitential practice in any event. For Flannery, the rules of the Church were not to be taken lightly. Thus, when a friend who was a "lapsed Catholic" sought Flannery's advice about the consequences of breaking them, Flannery alerted Father McCown. She explained that a priest had told this friend that eating meat on Friday constituted a mortal sin. Flannery wanted to set the record straight for her friend, who apparently refused to see a priest on her own. Although the friend's name is never divulged in the letters to Father McCown, it seems clear from other correspondence that she was her writer-friend Cecil Dawkins.

Of course, Flannery would have been well aware of the definition of a mortal sin as explained in the *Baltimore Catechism*. Such a transgression must involve grave matter and full consent of the will. Referencing her friend, Flannery posed an interesting theological question to Father McCown: "Would eating meat on Friday be a mortal sin if she didn't understand it as an act of rebellion?"[36] This question probes the distinction between *intentionally* breaking a rule as a way to rebel against Christ, and disregarding it for other reasons.

In his reply, Father McCown apparently reminded her that a mortal sin had to involve a deliberate act of rebellion. On January 12, 1958, she thanked him, while also mentioning her own struggles with her conscience. At times it was hard for her to decide what was sinful and what was not, since, "You can never so well decide if a thing is deliberate or not." Unknowingly proving Father McCown's observation about her "delicacy of conscience," Flannery also worried about having overlooked serious sins in past confessions: "You begin to wonder if your confessions have been adequate and if you are compounding sin on sin."[37]

This was a worrisome train of thought, headed towards an agonizing scrupulosity, but she stopped it mid-tracks with some self-directed humor. Flannery came to realize she was being too analytical, and she suggested that her fretting resulted from childhood experiences with the sisters, who had taught children "to measure... sins with a slide rule." She jokingly told her spiritual director that the tendency to be overly analytical drove "some folks nuts and some folks to the Baptists." She assured him that she would not take the latter option.

Going to Hell over Butterbeans

The fish-on-Friday rule comes up again in Flannery's letters. In December of 1959, she told Dawkins, "We are all bound by the Friday abstinence." The sin, she pointed out, resulted not from eating the meat but "in refusing the penance." She continued, "The sin is in disobedience to Christ, who speaks to us through the Church." Deliberately missing Mass on Sunday, she noted, was a similar act of disobedience.[38]

Then there was the butterbeans incident. It seems that Flannery and her mother had eaten at a restaurant on a Friday, and Flannery had ordered the vegetable plate. As she was eating, she suspected that the vegetables had been cooked in ham stock, but she was a frugal soul and wanted to get her money's worth, so she cleaned her plate anyway. After the meal, however, the waiter confirmed her suspicions.

"I know I ain't going to hell over a plate of butterbeans," she wrote to Father McCown on January 7, 1960, "but I don't know if I have to run to confession before I go to

Communion." Affirming again her deep reverence for the Eucharist, she added, "I am always afraid of sacrilege."[39]

Lukewarm Sermons

Butterbeans might be joked about, but Flannery also had much more serious discussions with her spiritual director, often stemming from her misgivings about the Catholic clergy. She was concerned because some of her friends had left the Church, and they often blamed priests for leaving. Perhaps in reference to Dawkins, she told Father McCown on December 23, 1958, "They have all left because they have been shocked by the intellectual dishonesty of some Catholic or other – or so they say, frequently of priests."[40]

Flannery went on to criticize priests who delivered lukewarm sermons, offering over-simple solutions to complex problems. She couldn't abide trite, predictable preaching, and as she confided to Father McCown, she wished more priests would focus on "the harm we do from the things we do not face" and explore "all the questions that we give Instant Answers to." None of her friends – those "poor children" who had left the Church – were satisfied with platitudes. One woman had graduated from a Catholic grammar school, but when Flannery sent her a good book by an abbot, the woman expressed amazement that a Catholic writer could be so intellectually flexible. "Apparently she has met nothing but idiot priests all her life, also idiot nuns."[41]

At another time, Flannery wrote Father McCown about a married Protestant friend who was interested in the Catholic faith and curious about the Church's position on contraception. The local priest in the woman's town had provided literature that apparently horrified the woman. As Flannery noted darkly, the material had no theological basis, "just all this junk about how great it is to be a mother." Although Flannery does not expand on the topic in this letter, it is clear from other letters that she fully accepted the Church's teachings on contraception and had little patience with what she called the "typical liberal" view. As she put it, Catholics had to find another solution to the population problem because they "can't think of birth control in relation to expediency but in relation to the nature of man under God."[42]

Flannery thanked Father McCown for sending her a copy of *Catholic Mind,* which contained an article "Theology and Population," which intelligently explained Church teaching. Describing it as "the best I've read on that subject," she told him she had sent her friend a copy of the article, which "should set things straight."[43]

With Crooked Lines

Even as friends turned their backs on the Catholic religion because of an unfortunate encounter with a misinformed priest, Flannery understood that the Church was more than the sum of its human parts. Years after her death, Father McCown wrote a book about his life, entitled *With Crooked Lines*, which included a story about his father and the Church that beautifully underscores the big picture of the Catholic faith. It is a tale that we can easily picture him having shared with Flannery at Andalusia. Father McCown recalls talking with his father about a priest who had disappointed the family. When the senior McCown called the man a "damn crook," the younger chimed in, saying that such priests almost made him want to leave the Catholic Church. But this comment seriously upset his father: "Don't you forget that the Church is the church of Jesus Christ," he replied angrily. "He founded it. He guides it. And he guarantees that it will always teach the truth."[44]

Human beings run the Church, the elder McCown reminded his son, and with people come problems. Such people "are not the Church," he said. "They are people in the Church." But their existence doesn't change the central truth: "Half the bishops, monsignors, and priests in the country, even the pope, could be crooked... and it wouldn't make a damn bit of difference."[45]

Church's imperfect members (handwritten margin note)

Defending the Clergy

It is not that surprising that Flannery, at times, made comments in letters that could be branded anti-clerical. She could be sharply critical of certain members of the clergy, just as she was towards certain Catholic prayers and publications. However, the weight of the evidence in her letters suggests that she was not fundamentally anti-clerical. Indeed, when the occasion called for it, Flannery could shape eloquent defenses of the clergy.

For example, writing on August 19, 1959, to Professor Ted R. Spivey, a Protestant, Flannery defended priests against attacks by one of his Catholic acquaintances. This person had complained about priests being "neurotic," an accusation that Flannery easily handled. Neurosis, by definition, was an illness and thus not something freely chosen, she explained, so it was wrong to condemn someone for it. She went on to defend the priesthood by affirming that it took a strong person to meet its responsibilities. Priests take lifelong vows, she reminded Spivey, and there are "very few defections." Yes, priests had failings, she admitted, but most of the ones she knew were "unimaginative and overworked," rather than neurotic.[46]

Perhaps as a result of her friendships with the Jesuits, Flannery was similarly quick to defend the clergy against other unfair attacks. She was aware of the burdens placed on priests, who represent the Church to the world in everything they do, and she recognized how easily lay people could mistake a priest's personal opinions for official Church teaching. As she noted, "No matter what he says in the way of his own opinion, people are going to take it for the Church speaking so that there is such a responsibility laid on him to begin with that he can hardly get off the ground."[47]

Father Finn from Purgatory

Although Flannery did not write her stories to promulgate positive messages about Catholicism, in her two stories that contain Catholic priests, both characters are good, solid clergymen who provide a moral compass. In "The Displaced Person," a Catholic priest reminds the main character that her decision to fire a Polish refugee, a worker on her farm, echoes the crowd's rejection of Jesus before the crucifixion. On each of his visits, he emphasizes her moral obligation to take care of the man and his family, an obligation that she ultimately ignores. After the man's tragic death, in which she is implicated, it is only the priest who comes to visit her.

"The Enduring Chill" also contains a priest who has keen insight into the central character's underlying problems. Although he is a non-believer, when he comes to fear that he's dying, Asbury asks his mother to call for a priest. He's hoping for a visit from a Jesuit, since he thinks of them as well-educated and interesting, but the cleric who appears at his bedside is the elderly, down-to-earth Father Finn, who seems to be modeled on a priest Flannery met at a luncheon.[49] Father Finn tells Asbury, tongue in cheek and with an Irish brogue, that he comes "from Purrgatory."

Rather than engage Asbury in a witty debate, Father Finn asks him basic questions about his prayer habits and his knowledge of the catechism. Asbury, who believes God is as "an idea created by man," becomes infuriated by the priest's seemingly simplistic approach, but in fact this no-nonsense priest is able to achieve what the doctors cannot: he gets to the heart of Asbury's deeper illness, which is spiritual.

✠ ✠ ✠ ✠

Flannery's most impassioned defense of the priesthood is seen in a letter to Dawkins dated December 9, 1958. There, she pointed out how easy it is to criticize priests: any child can pick out the faults in a sermon on his way home from Sunday Mass. She went on to say, however, that it was impossible for that same child to understand the "hidden love that makes a man, in spite of his intellectual limitations, his neuroticism, his own lack of strength, give up his life to the service of God's people, however bumblingly he may go about it."[50]

The woman who wrote these words cannot be called anti-clerical. On the contrary, Flannery's words reveal a deep understanding of, and love for, what the priesthood at heart is all about, which is modeling the sacrificial love of Jesus Christ.

· CHAPTER 9 · ≪

Integrated and Lapped with
Azaleas: Overcoming Racism

*A*mong critics much ink has flowed debating the question
of whether Flannery was a racist. One typical accusation described her letters as revealing a "habit of bigotry,"[1] and
said that she delighted in the white South's "dehumanizing"
manners.[2] This is clearly a question that bears on her spirituality, because Catholic teaching condemns racism, emphasizing Christ's precept to love our neighbors as ourselves. There
is of course the deeper question of whom we consider to be
our "neighbor"; obviously, many whites in her day did not see
black people in this light. Did Flannery?

   Unfortunately, some of Flannery's letters are peppered
with the ugly word "nigger," and for many people today that's
enough to brand her a racist. However, a careful reading of
her letters reveals that her use of this word belied her deeper
feelings about blacks and her real response to the racial integration taking place in the South. It is also important to

137

remember that, as her friend Sally Fitzgerald put it, Flan-
nery's tongue could take on an "unsaintly edge."³ Although
Fitzgerald didn't mention the "n" word per se, she clearly was
alluding to it when she wrote that her friend used "the pre-
vailing locution of the South as easily, and as unmaliciously,
as it often occurs there, among blacks and whites alike."⁴

With Crooked Lines

The relationship between Flannery and her Jesuit
spiritual director sheds some light on the mystery sur-
rounding her racial attitudes. Father McCown hailed
from Mobile, Alabama, and thus shared Flannery's very
Southern roots. When he met her in 1956, he already had
established his reputation as a radical in his day, since
he was strongly in favor of integration. As we have seen,
Flannery respected his views on theology and other matters, and it seems highly likely that she was well aware
of his strong opinions on race.

He no doubt had told her about his attempts to
establish an integrated parish in Fort Valley, Georgia, in
1953, three years before they'd met. The effort succeeded,
but when the completely integrated church opened, not
everyone was thrilled. In fact, as he noted in his book *With
Crooked Lines*, several of the most prominent white fami-
lies left the parish, and the losses were painful to him.
Thirty-seven years later, however, when he was writing
his book, he happily reported that the parish still was
thriving, and it remained the only racially integrated
house of worship in the vicinity.⁵

In that book, Father McCown explores the racial
atmosphere of pre-civil-rights days in the South. Although
he was fourteen years older than Flannery, these reflections give us valuable insights into her attitudes. He

grew up in Mobile in the early 1920s, and he admits that his childhood was permeated with racism. The word "colored" was considered the kindly term to use in reference to black people. "Negro" could be used with educated blacks, as long as you were careful not to say "nigra." If the McCown children slipped and said "nigger," their parents corrected them, but the underlying problem remained: the social climate in the South dictated that white children did not associate with black. Father McCown's childhood education, as Flannery's would be, was strictly segregated.[6]

Steeped in Racism

Father McCown's words ring with honesty and remorse when he admits that all the black people he knew were either uneducated servants or their children. Thus he bought into the harmful stereotype that blacks, as a race, were naturally less intelligent than whites.[7] He also mentions that it was considered standard for blacks to call white men "sir," whereas whites called black men, no matter what their ages, by their first names. "Nigger" jokes were plentiful at the time, as were blackface minstrel shows. Father McCown admits sadly that there was no one to tell him that "these stereotypes were hurtful and embarrassing to the blacks."[8]

Father McCown may not have used the "n" word as Flannery did, but he still concludes that "In my youth, in the South, we were steeped in racism." As he gradually became aware of the deeply rooted problems with his early upbringing, he underwent a change of heart. But he describes his family and friends as having been "imprisoned by [racism's] intricate inconsistencies."[9]

The Supposedly Liberal Newspaper

Flannery's early life may have been steeped in racism too, but like her spiritual director she was capable of rising above her background. Various incidents evidence this. In 1958, two years after meeting Father McCown, an editor at the *Atlanta Journal-Constitution* refused to review a book by her friend Brainard ("Lon") Cheney. Annoyed, she wrote an acquaintance at the newspaper to find out why, and then reported back to Cheney on October 12, 1958. The book editor was quoted as saying, "Sorry, honey, but it was about niggers." Flannery replied to Cheney, "This seems a trifle odd for the supposedly liberal *Constitution*."[10]

Cheney investigated the matter further, discovering that the editor had thought the author of the book was black. Still, even when he discovered that Cheney was white, the editor nixed the review because the plot featured blacks.[11] Writing to Cheney on October 24, Flannery suggested a solution. She advised him to send the book to the publisher, Ralph McGill.[12] In that same letter, she mentioned that a friend had spotted a favorable review of Cheney's book in a New York newspaper. Dispensing with the "n" word, she politely described the reviewer as a "very nice Negro whom I met at Yaddo."[13] Cheney took her sensible advice, and his book subsequently was reviewed by the publisher himself.

Devil's Advocate

Few people who accuse Flannery of racism seem to be aware of this incident involving the book editor. Instead, critics usually point to letters she wrote to her friend Maryat Lee. Born in Kentucky, Lee was a playwright living in New York City when her correspondence with Flannery began. The letters show that Lee had thrown herself into the civil rights movement with great fervor. They also reveal Flannery's use of racist language. In one letter to Lee, written on February 24, 1957, Flannery mentions talking at an event at Emory University, where a man said he was working with a group on "interpersonal relations." When someone asked him to define this term, she tells Lee that one of the other novelists there had said, "He means niggers and white folks."[14] In another letter, she mentions one proposed "solution" to the black-white problem: sending "them all back to Africa."[15]

Even these remarks have to be taken into context. As Ralph C. Wood points out, offhand opinions in letters can be quite different from convictions:

> We often keep our opinions to ourselves, lest they give needless offense, and lest we be made ashamed at their disclosure. Convictions, by contrast, are slowly acquired and firmly maintained. We do not surrender our convictions readily nor keep them private, no matter whom they may offend. They are the public verities upon which we stand, the truths by which we live and die.[16]

There is a story of Flannery's that nicely exemplifies this distinction, and also reveals what can happen when one reveals one's deep-set convictions about a subject as controversial as black-white relations. In "Revelation," a "white trash" woman sitting with a group in a doctor's waiting room shares aloud the proposed "solution" of sending blacks back to Africa. Another woman, Mrs. Turpin, who appears to be better educated, chimes in by explaining that this won't work, given the numbers of blacks presently in the United States. She goes on to air her own deeply racist views by suggesting that the goal of black persons is to "improve their color" by marrying white folks. It is not too long after this that Mary Grace, a student from Wellesley College, hurls a book across the room and clips Mrs. Turpin on the head.

In her letters to Lee, Flannery at times takes on the persona of an ignorant Southern white woman – akin to the unnamed lady in the waiting room – who harbors a cache of racist beliefs. But, as Wood has pointed out, when writing to Lee, Flannery seemed to enjoy exaggerating – even caricaturing – her own conservative, Southern views to contrast with her liberal, Northern friend's "Yankee" ideas.[17] According to Sally Fitzgerald, Lee was well aware of the good-natured sparring, and she indulged in it herself. In fact, Lee herself came to Flannery's defense on the racism charge, writing to Fitzgerald to explain that "Flannery permanently became devil's advocate with me in matters of race, as I was to do with her in matters of religion."[18]

Troubled Times

Despite the joking tone of the letters, running beneath the surface there was a serious discussion of how to solve the problems of race relations in the South. Lee was more inclined to dispense with social niceties and customs in order to achieve rapid social change, but Flannery was not. This may have been because Flannery was more aware than her "Yankee friend" of the social repercussions of going against the tide in small-town Georgia. For example, on January 9, 1957, she suggested that Lee had committed a big social blunder by being driven to the Atlanta airport by a black gardener.[19] Regina had even worried that if rumors about the incident spread around town, they could prove harmful to Lee's brother, who was then president of Georgia State College for Women in Milledgeville.

In that same letter, Flannery vividly described the backlash that often resulted when events ruffled the feathers of local segregationists. She told Lee of the time a past president of the college invited two blacks to attend a meeting there. She said that "everything was as separate and equal as possible, even down to two Coca-Cola machines, white and colored." Still, area racists were so enraged when they got wind of the meeting that they burned a cross on the president's lawn. (Flannery, who couldn't resist taking a sarcastic swipe at this crowd, said that for people who hadn't gone beyond fourth grade, the cross burners certainly seemed interested in education.) Flannery was even more concerned about possible repercussions for Lee because, "Those times weren't as troubled as these."[20] Writing to Lee on January 31, 1957, Flannery warned that the time Lee next visited, the "local backwoodsmen" – Milledgeville's Klan members – might stage a cross burning on the lawn of the Governor's Mansion.[21]

Anti-Catholicism in the South

Living as a Catholic in the Bible Belt, Flannery was no stranger to the dangerous and harmful effects of another kind of prejudice. Thus, we may view her resistance to abrupt social change in race relations as a kind of prudence, given Southern history, rather than as cowardice or apathy. Since her maternal great-grandfather, born in Ireland, became Milledgeville's first Catholic resident in 1833, it is highly likely that he and other relatives had passed down stories about anti-Catholic sentiment in

Georgia. Although she does not discuss anti-Catholicism in her letters, it is a definite thread running through many chapters of Southern history.

In *A Literary Guide to Flannery O'Connor's Georgia*, Sarah Gordon and Craig Amason give the unsavory historical details. Catholics were not even allowed to settle in Georgia before the Revolutionary War. They were granted some rights in the state constitution of 1777, but were still unable to hold political office. And it wasn't until 1789 that Catholics achieved equal rights under Georgia law. Despite these gains, Catholics in Georgia continued struggling for acceptance well into the twentieth century.[22] In fact, even as Catholics were granted more freedoms under the law, they were still subject to social biases – including vicious attacks by the Ku Klux Klan, which targeted not only blacks but also Catholics and Jews.

Flannery reveals the ugly thread of Southern anti-Catholicism very deftly in her fiction by placing such sentiments in the mouths of particularly ignorant characters. In *Wise Blood*, Hoover Shoates, also known as Onnie Jay Holy, conveys a typical small-town mistrust of Catholicism when he defends his church as having "nothing foreign" connected with it. He also assures listeners that they can interpret the Bible as they see fit and they "don't have to believe nothing [they] don't understand and approve of."[23]

Flannery shows the deadly effects of anti-Catholic prejudice in her story "The Displaced Person." In it a farm worker named Mr. Shortley and his wife both fear the presence of the priest who brings a Catholic Polish family (the Guizacs) to the farm. The backwoods Mr. Shortley predicts that the "Pope of Rome" will soon be dictating what happens on the farm. The equally ignorant Mrs.

Shortley expresses suspicion of a religion that goes back "a thousand years" and has never "advanced or reformed."[24] Even the more-educated farm owner, Mrs. McIntyre, harbors her own prejudices against the Catholic priest and the Polish family. The anti-Catholic prejudice erupts tragically when Mr. Guizac is fixing a tractor and another tractor starts rolling down the hill toward him. Rather than warn him, Mrs. McIntyre keeps silent, and watches the man die.

"Land of Sin and Guilt"

This story also shows how anti-Catholicism can go hand in hand with racism. Mrs. McIntyre had been horrified to discover that Mr. Guizac was trying to bring his cousin over from a Polish refugee camp to marry one of her black farm workers. Mr. Guizac assures her that the cousin, who has been in the camp three years, doesn't care that the worker is black. However, Mrs. McIntyre insists that the plans be dropped because of her racist conviction that blacks and whites should not marry.

Other Southern social customs mirrored this deep-seated fear of black-white intermarriage. We get a glimpse of these in the letters in 1959, when Lee told her Milledgeville friend that black author James Baldwin was traveling to Georgia, and Flannery should arrange to meet him. Today, this would seem like a small matter indeed, but it was a big deal at the time. And so Flannery set her Northern friend straight about the manners of the Deep South in 1959: "In New York it would be nice to meet him; here it would not." Such a meeting, she added, would cause "the greatest trouble and disturbance and disunion" in a Southern town. "Might as well expect a mule to fly," she added. Flannery had admired one of

Baldwin's stories and might have enjoyed meeting him. However, she accepted the reality of life in Milledgeville and didn't apologize to Lee for following the town's Southern customs. "I observe the traditions of the society I feed on – it's only fair."[25]

She does not specify the traditions, but it seems clear that she was referring to inviting him into her home to share a meal. And although she comes across as quite curt and matter of fact in these remarks to Lee, Flannery's good friend William Sessions reported many years later that Flannery had expressed "considerable anguish" to him about not being able to receive Baldwin in her home.[26] It is highly possible that Regina had balked at the notion of having a black man come to supper, and Flannery had given in. After all, according to Sessions, when Flannery became close friends with a black woman during her graduate-school days at the University of Iowa, it was Regina who protested that interracial contacts were "dangerous." The young Flannery had held her ground, saying that her "friendships would not be fettered by racial considerations,"[27] but the older Flannery was much more dependent on Regina, and no doubt was more inclined to bow to her rules.

In the spring of 1962, Flannery advised Lee to visit the South so she might get a dose of reality. Assuming the usual sparring tone of their letters, she noted that Lee could save money on the return trip by letting the "White Citizens Council" send her back: "You could tell them that you was a little light but a guaranteed nigger." Following this advice, she told Lee, would reduce Lee's expenses, while also giving her "a nice vacation in the land of sin and guilt." Flannery's tone turned suddenly melancholy as she admitted her true feelings: "I wish this wasn't for real and then I could have made it up."[28]

Conversion on the Bus

Flannery, like many other Southerners, indulged at times in rather shoddy racist jokes. In *The Habit of Being,* Fitzgerald wisely omitted a particular letter written to Hester that contained an unfortunate example of this Southern habit. However, the original letter can be found in the cache held in the Emory University archives. In that missive, Flannery shared a racist story told by a handyman at Andalusia. According to this fellow, whom Flannery described as "poor white aristocracy," a person drinking a Pepsi Cola had discovered a piece of overalls in it. Subsequently, the Pepsi people had discovered that a black man (although, unfortunately, this was not the word the storyteller used) had somehow fallen into a vat of the soft drink in Macon.[29]

We might wonder why Flannery would have made the effort to type out such a banal story. In her defense, letters served as a form of conversation for her. Although a telephone had been installed at Andalusia a year earlier, she was more inclined to "chat" in letters. A crude story such as this, related over the telephone, might have elicited a groan from the listener and then quickly been forgotten. In a letter, unfortunately, it was preserved for generations to come.

However, a letter penned by this same woman only three months later would seem to exonerate her. There, Flannery wrote about a past experience that had brought her face to face with the real-life suffering endured by blacks in a segregated society. Her moment of personal conversion had taken place on a bus, she reported, when the driver had told the rear occupants, who, of course, were black, "All right, all you stove-pipe blonds, git on back ther." In this letter dated November 16, 1957, Flannery told Hester in no uncertain terms that, right then and there, she had experienced a change of heart: "I became an integrationist."[30]

Outside Agitators

Five years after she wrote her letter about the experience on the bus, the racial situation in Milledgeville became more volatile still. On August 9, 1962, Flannery reported to Cheney that the town had experienced its first attempted sit-in, at a local drugstore. She told him that a neighbor had reported to Flannery and her mother that a "carful of nigger sports" in Bermuda shorts had stopped at the "negro café." When they sent a black woman around to check out the scene at the drugstore, she reported a surprise. It seems news about the sit-in had leaked, and the drugstore owner had rallied the "local backwoodsmen."

The scene at the drugstore was right out of a Flannery O'Connor story. Based on the neighbor's report, Flannery described the place to Cheney as jam-packed with "the toughest folks the county could produce." They stayed there all day, brandishing their switch-blade knives, and reading newspapers and comic books. Flannery noted ironically that some "had never been known to read before." The sit-in folded, but that night the Ku Klux Klan met across the road from Andalusia, striking fear into the hearts of local blacks. Flannery noted sadly that "our colored man," one of the workers at Andalusia, had left town that very night. "I hate to see it all get started," she added.[31] Her words clearly reveal her dislike not only of the ignorance and intimidation of the Klan, but also of the turmoil that sit-ins and demonstrations brought to a small Southern town.

Yes, Flannery had declared herself an integrationist after her experience on the bus, but she still favored slow, rather than dramatic, social changes, largely because of her concern about backlash. Writing in 1963 to Janet McKane, the schoolteacher who lived in New York City, Flannery reported that some blacks in Milledgeville had petitioned the city council to integrate the schools, restaurants, and library. Unbeknownst to them, however, the library had been quietly integrated the year before. For Flannery, the library situation exemplified change coming about quietly, without publicity – and without trouble.[32]

Integrated and Lapped with Azaleas

Over the years, Flannery became increasingly more supportive of integration. At one of her speaking engagements, at Spring Hill College in Mobile, she experienced firsthand a good example of peaceful co-existence between blacks and whites. On April 10, 1960, she made a favorable report about the experience to Cheney. "They begin their classes with Our Father, close them with the Hail Mary, are integrated and lapped with azaleas."[33] A few years later, Flannery admitted to Lee that she admired the goals of Martin Luther King, Jr. Although she did not revere him as the "age's great saint," she did, however, express faith in his goals by affirming that he was doing "what he can do & has to do."[34] We don't know if she ever read his "Letter from a Birmingham Jail," composed in 1963. She might have shown even more admiration for King had she realized that he had studied one of her favorite saints, Thomas Aquinas, and in his letter had appealed to Thomistic principles.

Lost in Atlanta

Flannery's short story "The Artificial Nigger," despite a racist-sounding title that caused controversy in its time and still does today, reveals her sympathy for the suffering of blacks in the South perhaps better than anything else she ever wrote. It features the backwoods Mr. Head, who wants to take Nelson, his 10-year-old grandson, to visit Atlanta, so the boy can witness the bleakness of the big city and be content to stay at home in their small town. Nelson has never even seen a black man, and Mr. Head assures him he won't like Atlanta because it's "full of niggers." After the twosome gets lost in the black part of Atlanta, the grandfather decides to demonstrate how important he is in the child's life by pretending to leave the boy behind. When Nelson loses sight of the grandfather, he becomes so terrified that he plows into a crowd, knocking down an elderly woman. The police show up and want Mr. Head to assume responsibility for the boy's behavior, but the old man does the unthinkable: he denies that the child is his kin.

It is after this terrible moment of betrayal – which in a letter Flannery compared to St. Peter's denial of Christ – that the twosome comes across the plaster figure of a black man. The statue is unsteady, its putty cracked, its eye chipped, and the watermelon it holds is brown. They can't tell the age of the artificial man, since it looks "too miserable" to be young or old. As they stand gazing at it, their moment of grace comes: they see it as "the monument to another's victory" and feel it "dissolving their differences like an action of mercy."[35] The grandfather understands for the first time what mercy feels like, and also realizes, for the first time, that he is a sinner. The "artificial nigger" awakens in Mr. Head the first feelings of sympathy for what blacks have endured in the South, and saves him from his sinful pride.

Commenting on this story, Flannery said that nothing encapsulated the tragedy of the South so much as what her uncle called "nigger statuary."[36] She told Father McCown that the broken statue was a "terrible symbol" of what the South had done to itself,[37] and told another friend that it symbolized the "redemptive quality of the Negro's suffering for us all."[38]

Grace and Mutual Charity

In 1963, about eight years after that story was published in *A Good Man Is Hard to Find,* and a year before her death, Flannery expressed strong support for the civil rights movement while also applauding the gains already made in black-white relations. She expressed approval of "those changes in the South that have been long overdue—the whole racial picture." She went on to say that the situation was improving, especially in Georgia, and added that she felt good about that.[39] As Ralph C. Wood points out, this statement definitely refutes "the mocking claims" in her letters to Lee.[40]

Flannery's own words should put to rest forever the notion that she was truly a racist. They are strengthened by the comment of Fitzgerald, who said, without qualification, "Her will was never in danger on the score of racism."[41] It is true that Flannery had a different take on the race situation from her friend Lee. Flannery believed the problems in the South wouldn't be *entirely* solved by passing laws, but instead required a change in behavior, a change in culture. Interviewed in 1963, she said the South had to evolve "a way of life in which the two races [could] live together with mutual forbearance." This would require "considerable grace" and a code of manners based on mutual charity.[42]

She would no doubt agree that we can legislate the ways people receive education, the places they can go, and the things they are allowed to do. But we can't pass laws requiring people of different races to see each other as neighbors. We can't require them to be charitable to each other or to love each other as Christ loves them. This change of heart, above all else, requires God's powerful intervention in the hearts of men. As Flannery remarked in a 1958 letter to Dawkins, the South "still believes that man has fallen and that he is only perfectible by God's grace, not by his own unaided efforts."[43]

✠   ✠   ✠   ✠

Flannery was by no means perfect. She knew she was a sinner, and on matters of race she was to some degree a product of her time and place. But those who damn her as a racist because of exaggerated remarks in her letters, or because her characters use slurs common in the 1950's rural South, miss the chance to examine the full range of evidence.

They fail to see, for example, that Flannery was certainly not a racist in the theological sense; she would never have denied that blacks and whites were all God's children and could all be redeemed by the blood of Christ. They ignore the fact that, although she was not one to favor marches, sit-ins, or shocking breaches of social convention, Flannery did do her part, in her quiet, monastic way, to stem the tide of racism by revealing in her stories its ugly underbelly. In her particularly Catholic approach to suffering, she recognized that no agony is ever meaningless, and believed thus that blacks had not suffered in vain, any more than Christ had, because, as she showed in her stories, out of suffering can come a change of heart – and redemption.

This is seen in "Everything That Rises Must Converge," when a young man named Julian has a final awakening, realizing that his mother, despite what he sees as her embarrassing attitude towards racial matters (she calls a black child a "pick-a-ninny") truly loved the black nanny who had raised her, whereas he, a self-righteous, arrogant advocate of racial equality, is incapable of loving his own mother. It is also seen in "Revelation," where Mrs. Turpin, a racist in the process of conversion, has a vision in which a crowd of souls is marching toward heaven. "White trash" and blacks head the procession with well-off whites like her husband and herself trailing behind them. It's little wonder that in her vision the faces of the respectable white people are "shocked and altered" as what they thought were "virtues" are being burned away. It is this very process of being altered that stands for the conversion that has to take place in the heart before any real change can occur. It was this conversion that took place, over many years, in Flannery's own heart.

V

The Action of Grace

*H*e stood appalled, judging himself with the thoroughness of God, while the action of mercy covered his pride like a flame and consumed it.

—*"The Artificial Nigger"*

CHAPTER 10

A Reluctant Pilgrim: Journey to Lourdes

Many people would be thrilled at the offer of a free trip to visit the Marian shrine in Lourdes, France. However, getting there from the United States entails quite a bit of travel, and the place itself is overrun with tourists. Thus, when Flannery's elderly cousin, Katie, offered to treat her and Regina to a pilgrimage to Lourdes (where many go to seek miraculous healing), Flannery was less than ecstatic. She certainly wasn't averse to believing in miracles, but she was a very reluctant traveler. Besides, she found pilgrimages distracting: "My prayers are better said at home."[1]

Flannery finally did acquiesce to go on the trip, but she proclaimed strongly to her friends that there was no way on earth she would bathe in the Grotto's spring. That she finally took the plunge reveals an important feature of her faith: she came to see that believing in miracles on an abstract level wasn't enough. Her faith had to be put into practice, even if that meant sacrificing her squeamishness about pious devotions. As we shall see, her motives for taking the bath weren't perfect, but they were quite human, and her ability to overcome her reluctance may be taken as evidence of God's grace.

The Healing Spring

Flannery and her mother would have been well aware of the importance of Lourdes: how, in 1858, in the grotto of Massabielle, near Lourdes in southern France, a young peasant girl named Bernadette Soubirous claimed to have seen the Virgin Mary on eighteen different occasions. According to the child's report, Mary asked that a chapel be built on the site of the visions and also instructed the child to drink from a fountain in the grotto. No fountain then existed, but when the child started digging, a spring began to flow, which has continued flowing to this day, with water reputed to have healing powers. It is likely this part of the story really intrigued Cousin Katie, who, like Regina, would have been very concerned about Flannery's illness. And when Katie discovered that there was a diocesan pilgrimage being planned to Lourdes and Rome, she "insisted" that Regina and Flannery go, and at her own expense. Flannery reported that Regina was all for going, since, as Flannery put it, "this is about the only way either of us will ever get there."[2]

"A Comic Nightmare"

As a faithful Catholic, Flannery believed in miracles. She was well aware that miracles were "the great embarrassment for the modern man, a kind of scandal." However, if they could simply be argued away, she said, Christ would end up "reduced to the status of a teacher, domestic and fallible." And the very heart of Christianity would dwindle.[3]

It's likely, however, that Flannery would have retained a healthy skepticism about apparitions and other reported miraculous phenomena until the Church had made a ruling on them. After all, this is the woman who was not hesitant to express her dismay at St. Patrick's Day celebrations and devotions that she found sappy. But she surely knew that the Church had investigated the events at Lourdes a century before, and ruled that the Virgin Mary had indeed appeared to Bernadette. Since then, millions of people from all over the world have gone to Lourdes, hoping for a miracle. Some have received physical healing in the water, and others have found in it spiritual renewal. Flannery would have known this too, but she hated crowds and overt expressions of emotions, so she would have been understandably hesitant about joining the procession of pilgrims.

It is certainly an understatement to say that crowds weren't Flannery's great delight. She generally disdained cities, preferring the peaceful solitude of Andalusia. She was well aware of the throngs eagerly flocking to shrines, so it's not surprising that she tried her best to avoid making the pilgrimage. Indeed, Flannery viewed the prospect of the "seventeen-day" trip, originally scheduled for April 22 to May 7, 1958, as a "comic nightmare."[4] Along with eschewing crowds, Flannery dreaded the prospect of getting into the water in public, a maneuver that would have been especially awkward with the crutches that she was using.

Holy Exhaustion

It is clear from numerous letters that Flannery truly dreaded the journey, but her descriptions are hilarious nonetheless. In a letter to Hester, she imagined a planeload of "fortress-footed female Catholics pushed from shrine to shrine." She decided the best course of events would be to "cut my motor off... and be towed."[5] On November 4, 1957, she wrote to the Fitzgeralds, telling them she expected to find Catholic females "herded from holy place to holy place by the Rev. McNamara to the point of holy exhaustion."[6]

In that same letter, she mentioned that "I don't know whether I am expected to wash my bones in the waters [of Lourdes] or not; that don't interest me in the least." In her estimation, having to stay on crutches was preferable to such humiliation. "The lack of privacy would be what I couldn't stand," she admitted frankly. "This is neither right nor holy of me but it is what it is."[7] So she assured Hester that she was going as a pilgrim, not a patient, and she unabashedly described herself as the sort of person who "could die for his religion easier than take a bath for it." In fact, she said, washing in someone else's blood might be preferable to public bathing.

A few months later, it appeared that she had gotten a reprieve. On February 12, 1958, she told Dawkins the trip was off because her doctors thought it would be too strenuous for her: "I am just as well satisfied, as I was not looking forward to the exertion."[8] Her relief, however, was short-lived. A mere two weeks later, she told friends that Cousin Katie had been so disappointed that Flannery and her mother had caved in: "[Katie] says we must go anyway and not stay with the tour.[9]

An Appropriate Penance

In the end, it was decided that mother and daughter would go to Lourdes, but on a shorter tour than originally planned. Instead of journeying to Ireland and England, they would head to Milan, where they would meet the Fitzgeralds and spend four or five days. Then mother and daughter would fly to Paris and "join the pilgrims – of which there will be only twelve," Flannery noted on April 14, 1958. After that, they would travel to Lourdes, Barcelona, Rome, and Lisbon, and arrive home on May 8. "You'll probably never catch me out of the confines of the United States again," Flannery remarked.[10]

Hall, who was then the book editor at *The Bulletin*, inadvertently added to the comedy of the situation by saying she hoped that while at Lourdes, Flannery would discover a vocation to the Marist Third Order. Flannery relayed this to Hester with characteristic wryness: "All I can say is boy, that would be an appropriate penance but I hope I'll be spared."[11]

The Devil's Answer to the Virgin Mary

The trip proved even worse than Flannery had imagined. Writing Hester on May 5, 1958 from Rome, she reported that she had been plagued by an infection, and was taking whatever medicine that the pilgrimage leader, the monsignor, happened to have with him. She also described her traveling companions as consisting of four old ladies who were always getting lost, four priests, two little boys (aged twelve and fourteen), two secretaries, and "me and ma."[12] All this, she said, she was "enduring more or less."

Flannery noted that one of the secretaries was a red-headed lady from Albany, Georgia, who was about twenty-six and wore three-inch-high heels. Her main interest was shopping. "The lady made a purchase at every stop," and when asked about going to see the cathedral at Barcelona, "She groaned and said, 'Seen one,

seen em all.'" A little woman from Savannah was likable
enough, Flannery remarked, although "she lacked a grain
of sense" and was terrified of flying. She took to carrying
a tin can of Lourdes water with her "and was always losing it, herself, everything else." The little boys on the trip
tortured the woman by asking her, every time the plane
dipped down, "Ready to crash?"[13]

The city of Lourdes itself was a commercial nightmare – "completely defaced by religious junk shops" –
with omnipresent vendors hawking tacky religious paraphernalia.[14] She remarked to a friend how Mauriac
had written that religious-goods shops were "the devil's
answer there to the Virgin Mary," adding, "It's apparent
that the devil has a good deal to answer to."[15]

Seeking the Supernatural

"Well, I did it all and with very bad grace," Flannery
reported to Hester.[16] To escape embarrassment, she had
gone early in the morning, when there were only about
forty people ahead of her in line. But she another concern:
hygiene. To her relief, the water looked pretty clean, but
we can imagine her face when she saw a communal cup
being passed around. "I had a nasty cold so I figured I left
more germs than I took away," she quipped to another
friend.[17] Also, before entering the water, bathers donned
a sack for modesty; however it seems that the sack was
"the same one the person before you took off, regardless
of what ailed him." After the experience, Flannery concluded, "The supernatural is a fact there but it displaces
nothing natural; except maybe those germs."[18]

William Sessions was studying abroad that year and
met Flannery, Regina, and Sally Fitzgerald at Lourdes.
He vividly recalled, many years after her death, the

expression on Flannery's face after she had taken the bath and was standing by watching the crowds. "She looked tired," he said, "but that same penetrating glance that could shape a whole social world in a doctor's waiting room with such irony and that could whirl a Georgia country boy into preaching with such violence swept those weary Lourdes faces with the same embrace."[19]

Flannery might have appreciated her friend's poetic description of her expression that day, but she eschewed any flowery descriptions about bathing at Lourdes. In fact, she strongly insisted to other friends that she deserved no credit for taking the plunge. She felt her motives were all wrong: she did it to avoid feeling guilty later, and to please her companions. Writing on May 17, she told Hester how Fitzgerald was determined that Flannery would bathe in the healing water. In fact, she noted darkly, Fitzgerald would give her no peace. "If I hadn't taken it she said it would have been a failure to cooperate with grace and me, seeing myself plagued in the future by a bad conscience, took it." In a footnote to this letter, Fitzgerald admitted that she was forceful about the situation, but she defended herself. She said that she didn't want Flannery later to feel that she had disappointed Cousin Katie. As Fitzgerald put it, "She knew I would insist and that was perhaps the reason she so much wanted me to come along."[20]

But however reluctantly, Flannery did cooperate with grace; only her prayers weren't for her physical health. On August 17, 1958, she told Father Watson the real story: "I prayed for my creative bones rather than the other kind." And then, in a line that reveals so much about her humility and compassion, she added: "The thing about Lourdes is that you are not inclined to pray there for yourself at all as you see so many people worse off."[21]

Meeting the Pope

The trip wasn't over after the bath. Instead, Flannery and her mother and the rest of the pilgrims headed to Saint Peter's for an audience with Pope Pius XII. In her May 5 letter to Hester, Flannery wrote that the Pope greeted them and shook their hands after his talk, and then complied with Archbishop O'Hara's request to give her a special blessing because of her crutches. She was greatly impressed with Pius XII, declaring that he had a wonderful radiance, despite his advanced age. "Whatever the special superaliveness that holiness is, it is very apparent in him."[22] The rest of the group subsequently went to Fatima, but Flannery and her mother declined because it would have been a long trip and poor Regina had a cold. Still, Flannery was relieved to have an excuse. "Shrines to the Virgin do not seem to increase my devotion to her and I was glad not to go."

On the way back to United States, the plane ride "about finished" her, she wrote, and then she went on to describe how one of the men kept falling asleep with his mouth open, and a little boy kept pretending to insert a coin in it. As for the ailing Regina, she "revived as soon as she hit the cow country."[23]

Was It a Miracle?

After all the jokes about the pilgrims and the trip, Flannery finally admitted another reason she took the bath. "It is obvious even to me that faith has to be shown, acted out," she wrote to Hester on May 31. Putting our faith into practice in the world often involves sacrifices, as the whole experience at Lourdes certainly had done for Flannery. Referencing the Old Testament practice of offering animals to God, she added: "We sacrifice time and vanity now instead of goats, which is really much harder."[24]

"Maybe this is Lourdes," Flannery wrote to another friend a few months later, after the doctor reported that her hip bone was stronger. He was even permitting Flannery to walk around the room without crutches, and Flannery expressed hope that if the improvement continued, she might no longer need them in a year or two. And even if the improvement was not due to a Lourdes miracle, she deemed it "something to be grateful to the same Source for."[25] Two days before Christmas that same year, she shared the good news with Father McCown, saying she was willing to ascribe the improvement either to Lourdes "or somebody's prayers."[26]

✠   ✠   ✠   ✠

There were other intangible benefits that resulted from the trip. A few months after Flannery and her mother returned, poor Cousin Katie became gravely ill, but before the old lady died, she had a moment of great joy: "She had the happiness of knowing that the trip to Lourdes has effected some improvement in my bones."[27] Meanwhile, Flannery continued to connect the healing at Lourdes with her writing. For example, when her second novel, *The Violent Bear It Away*, took a turn for the better, she wrote Father Watson on August 17, 1958, that her prayers at Lourdes were being answered.[28]

About five months later, she mentioned to Hester that she had finally completed a first draft of this book, which she had been working on for many years. She gave Lourdes more credit for this milestone than for the improvement in her health. "Anyway, it means more to me."[29]

CHAPTER 11

Genuine Works of the Lord: Andalusia's Birds and Beasts

lannery's reprieve from illness was short-lived, and she began to suffer more acutely from the side-effects of the medications she took to control the symptoms of lupus. One of the worst was the gradual and painful deterioration of her bones, especially in her jaw and hips. It became increasingly difficult for her to walk without crutches, and extremely taxing to leave Andalusia, except for essentials such as attending Mass and visiting doctors. But although the situation sounds grim, Andalusia provided many joys. Topping the list were the birds and beasts that made their home there.

Father McCown recalled that the gravel driveway leading to the O'Connor home was ruled by a large white swan. The bird was, he avowed, quarrelsome enough to be dangerous. On his very first visit to Andalusia, a peacock shrieked at him, a gaggle of geese hissed at him, and chickens scattered as he walked.[1] Of course, this rural setting was exactly what was required for Flannery's writing: it provided solitude and privacy, but also many opportunities to see – and hear – God's handiwork.

It was also a perfect setting for Flannery to indulge her lifelong fascination with birds. She often gave her friends peacock feathers as gifts, referring to them as "genuine works of the Lord." Surely it is telling that when she picked up a paint brush, her favorite subjects were chickens, guineas, and pheasants. And when she painted a self-portrait, she placed a pheasant cock at her side.[2] Seven months before her death, she had saved up enough money to get a record player, but decided to order a pair of swans instead.[3] This love for birds probably was not surprising to Regina. After all, as a little girl her daughter had attracted media attention by teaching her pet chicken how to walk backwards down the stairs in their Savannah home across from the cathedral.

God's Presence at Andalusia

For Flannery, there was a sacred quality to nature. Like Gerard Manley Hopkins, a favorite poet, she saw the world as "charged with the grandeur of God." No wonder she exulted in living away from the city, in a rural environment where the deafening sounds of civilization were blissfully absent. There were no cars, buses, trains, ambulances, or construction crews. Instead, she reveled in the screaming peacocks at night and a certain degree of squawking and clucking by day. The birds gave her a respite from writing, as well as a reason for laughing, even on the worst days.

Flannery expressed appreciation for William Faulkner's review of *The Old Man and the Sea*, especially his comparison of a fish's eye to a "saint in a procession." Writing to the Fitzgeralds, she said she was impressed by Faulkner's opinion that Hemingway had discovered God the Creator by writing that story.[4] With her own keen ability to perceive God's handiwork in the birds and beasts around her, at Andalusia Flannery was able to see a procession of saints every time she stepped outdoors, where "God is immediately present."[5]

As a Catholic, Flannery believed that God reveals himself in the natural world that he fashioned – a world which, although fallen and stained by Original Sin, remains God's creation, filled with many beauties and wonders. As she said in a talk delivered in 1963, a year before her death, "This physical, sensible world is good because it proceeds from a divine source."[6] Still, as much as Flannery saw God's face in her menagerie, and as much as she enjoyed writing letters detailing the latest in the lives of her ducks, swans, geese, burros, and, of course, the splendid peafowl, she never became overly sentimental about nature. Flannery knew that a bird was a bird, and a man was a man.

Her way of thinking was hierarchical and thoroughly Catholic. Human beings, created in God's image, stand at the pinnacle of creation, and they are charged with the responsibility of being good stewards of the lower forms of nature. "I believe that all creation is good," Flannery noted, "but that what has free choice is more completely God's image than what does not have it."[7] This point of view meant that Flannery never became unduly attached to her animals. The peafowl provided the occasional radiant feather to share with friends, while her other birds provided eggs. However, Flannery was practical. Yes, a goose might inspire funny stories for her letters, but there was also the likelihood that, at some point, the fellow might end up as her supper.

"Raising Ducks and Writing"

Flannery's role as steward to the birds at Andalusia (by the good graces of her mother, Regina, who took charge of the other beasts) was essential to her identity. "I am at present living in Milledgeville, Georgia, raising ducks and game birds, and writing," she noted jokingly to her editor.[8] She also told Hester that her avocation was raising peacocks, "something that requires everything of the peacock and nothing of me."[9] Indeed, the birds gave her a respite from the grind of writing and giving talks. For example, after Flannery was interviewed on a TV show, an experience she called "mildly ghastly," she rejoiced at returning to Andalusia, where she could be among her chickens, "who don't know I have just published a book."[10]

It is easy to imagine Flannery, her morning writing done, ambling outside to see what the birds were up to, then later reporting on their antics in her letters. There were her twenty-one brown ducks with blue wing bars, walking in single file everywhere they went.[11] When her fifteen turkeys came down with an ailment called "the sorehead," she painted black shoe polish on their heads so that they resembled "domesticated vultures," prancing about in "blackface."[12] Her two worlds collided when at one point she found herself sitting awkwardly at the typewriter, trying to write while two orphaned baby quail lay chirping in a box beneath her feet. "It is interfering with my powers of communication," she admitted dryly.[13] Then there was the turkey hen that hatched an egg that a goose had "surreptitiously" laid in its nest. Flannery thought the hen seemed embarrassed by the situation, but the tom resolved it: he killed the baby goose, thereby relieving his mate of "that perplexity."[14] Quoting Tennyson, Flannery told a friend that "Nature is red in tooth & claw."

"Do Those Things Eat Flowers?"

Anyone familiar with Flannery's fiction knows it contains scenes of startling horror side-by-side with uproarious comedy. This juxtaposition of laughter and tears is in keeping with a deep message of Catholicism: no matter how bad things get, we hope for a happy ending. The Crucifixion births the Resurrection; suffering gives way to joy. It had to have been a terrible shock for Flannery when in 1952 she realized she had lupus, the same illness that had killed her father. Still, instead of falling into a pit of misery, she did something that would over time bring her a great deal of joy. She sat down and perused the farmer's bulletin, then circled an ad for a peacock and a hen with four seven-week-old chicks.[15]

"I'm going to order me those," she informed her mother, who immediately shot back, "Do those things eat flowers?" Although they could not have known it then, the words were somewhat prophetic. Over the years, the birds would become a source of great delight for the daughter, and of great annoyance for the mother: for peafowl do indeed eat flowers, along with other plants. In any event, Flannery neatly sidestepped the question by assuring her mother that they would eat seeds.[16]

"She had always loved birds," noted Fitzgerald in 1991, many years after Flannery's death, "but the peacocks became special."[17] In an essay called "The King of Birds," Flannery described the especially thrilling moment when the peafowl first arrived from Florida: "As soon as the birds were out of the crate, I sat down on it and began to look at them," continuing to gaze at them ever since – "and always with the same awe."[18] Later she boasted happily to friends: "I am going to be the World Authority on Peafowl, and I hope to be offered a chair someday at the Chicken College."[19] She took special delight in describing one bird's trick, which consisted of running up to anyone smoking a cigarette and snatching it away. "He has eaten two hot [cigarettes] so far," she wrote proudly.[20]

The Misfit Bird

Andalusia presented some dangers to the peafowl: predators such as stray dogs, foxes, weasels, and mink, as well as parasitic worms.[21] It also could prove dangerous if a bird got too close to certain human beings. Flannery discovered this fact when a peacock lost a foot in a collision with a farm hand's sling blade. "The victim is doing fine," she assured Hester on May 18, 1957, "but I don't know what I am going to do with a one-legged peacock."[22]

Surely Hester realized the irony of the situation: The writer known for fictional grotesques now had a real-life misfit on her hands. For its safety the bird had to be separated from the others, Flannery told Hester in early June.[23] In a follow-on letter, she chided her friend for expressing sympathy for the "lonely" bird. Animals didn't have human emotions; as she told Hester, peafowl had only two special concerns: figuring out where their next meal was coming from, and avoiding anything that wanted to kill them until they could find something to kill.[24] By September, the handicapped bird had managed to be reabsorbed into the flock – and despite his infirmity, he was able to jump high enough to snitch food from the peahens.[25]

If there was any wonder about why Flannery kept these noisy birds that were prone to eating her mother's flowers, the answer is found in a scene recalled in an article by her spiritual director. Father McCown and Flannery were sitting on the front porch at Andalusia when suddenly a one-legged peacock appeared before them and manifested its "shattering peacock display." (Anyone who has seen such an event knows that a peacock goes from drab to astonishing in seconds.) Flannery turned to the priest, and in a whisper explained that in medieval times the peacock had been seen as "a symbol of the Transfiguration of Jesus." Father McCown evidently concurred with this interpretation, although he couldn't resist noting wryly in his reminiscence that the flamboyant birds could just as easily symbolize the sin of pride.[26]

"Amen!"

The peacock's impressive tail extends about four feet when fully opened, revealing "a galaxy of gazing, haloed suns."[27] For a peacock's whole life, Flannery wrote, "he will have nothing better to do than manicure it, furl and unfurl it, dance forward *and backward* with it spread, scream when it is stepped upon, and arch it carefully when he steps through a puddle." In her story "The Displaced Person," Flannery describes an old Irish priest's moment of awe when a peacock unfurls its tail, revealing "tiers of small pregnant suns" floating in a "green-gold haze." The priest is transfixed, "his jaw slack," and as he stands there, gaping, he pronounces, "Christ will come like that!"[28]

For real-life guests beholding one of Flannery's peacocks with its tail in full array, it was always a memorable moment. Some whistled, some became speechless, and one lady cried out, "Amen!"[29] But when a man who came to install a telephone at Andalusia in the summer of 1956 saw one fine peacock showing off its tail, he didn't say a word. Flannery thought he had been struck dumb by the bird's beauty. But then, in a moment right out of one of her stories, he drawled, "Longlegged rascal, ain't he? I bet he could outrun a Greyhound bus."[30]

Mother and Daughter and Birds

It turned out that Flannery had been partly correct about the peafowl's eating habits: they did indeed enjoy dining on seeds, but they also loved eating her mother's flowers, along with figs from her uncle's prized trees. Still, the fact that Regina allowed the troublesome animals to remain at Andalusia speaks volumes about her love for Flannery. She knew the birds were her daughter's delight, and this surely softened her heart. Still, she couldn't resist causing a big ruckus when the birds really got out of hand.

For example, in April of 1956, after a few peafowl had decimated a strawberry patch, Flannery told a friend that her mother was taking a dark view of the birds, such that it would be necessary to "reestablish relations between her and them."[31] The conflict between mother and daughter continued for years. In the summer of 1963, after her mother had installed a new feeder for Andalusia's calves, Flannery described how the peafowl had lined up to eat from it "like patrons at a diner." Regina complained that they had consumed $17.50 worth of calf feed in the past month, and now the geese were at it too.[32]

Fallout on Andalusia

Swans also held court at Andalusia. Writing to Hester on September 2, 1961, Flannery reported that a girl in

Florida had been searching for a pair of cheap swans to send her. The girl discovered a man selling swans for half price, but at $125 each, they were still too expensive for Flannery's pocketbook. Then, however, the girl found out that "the fellow had one pair that he would sell for $65 because the hen was blind in one eye."

"Of course this was for me," Flannery, said. When the pair arrived from Miami, Flannery was thrilled with the latest grotesque addition: "My cup runneth over."[33]

In that same letter, however, Flannery assumed a distinctively somber tone. The Cuban Missile Crisis had gripped the nation in fear, as Flannery and Regina could see on their recently acquired television (which made "all this very immediate"). Flannery confided to her friend that she was starting to believe, "We are headed for a cataclysm." Evidently she and Regina had spoken with a Civil Defense man about installing a fall-out shelter on the farm, and she described the talk as "not exactly cheering."

As she mulled over the horrendous possibility of a bomb falling, her thoughts turned to the havoc that would be wreaked upon nature. She quoted from the Book of Jonah: "And shall not I spare Nineveh, that great city, where there are over a hundred and twenty thousand persons that know not how to distinguish between their right hand and their left, *and many beasts.*" Her closing words were especially poignant, given how much she loved the animals at Andalusia: "I see the fallout settling on the cows and the peacocks and the swans."

Wedded to Habit

Future reports about the swans were more cheerful. In handwritten letters to Sister Julie, one of the nuns at Our Lady of Perpetual Help Home, Flannery provided a running commentary about these birds, joking about the male's peculiar habits and lamenting when the females failed to produce eggs.[34] A "moth-eaten pair," the swans were known for their strict adherence to routines. This behavior must have especially intrigued their owner, whose own writing and prayer regimens were deeply embedded. "They do the exact same thing every day," she told Hester on January 26, 1962. "They go down [to the pond] before breakfast... fish all morning, and [come] back promptly at 1 for the noon meal. They then stay up here for the afternoon and night." She added that she had never seen a set of birds "so wedded to habit."[35]

Although she had hoped that her two swans would nest before summer's end, when the one-eyed female swan died, Flannery accepted the disappointment in stride. Suspicious that the bird had not been the male's mate but its mother, she decided to find a younger female for him. Meanwhile, as she reported to Sister Julie on December 12, 1962, the male had taken up with three Muscovy ducks, "the only birds around here he's not scared of." He went to the pond with them and acted "like a large nursemaid trying to keep up with three lively children."[36] About ten months later, she sent Sister Julie a picture of the swan near a bird bath that she claimed he had fallen in love with.[37]

Little Spotted Mules

If peacocks reminded Flannery of the Transfiguration, she also had an animal that reminded her of the Crucifixion. It was a Sicilian burro named Marquita, which bore a mark on its back resembling a cross. According to Flannery, she was also the kind of burro that had carried Christ into Jerusalem. Adding burros to Andalusia, not surprisingly, had been Flannery's idea, not Regina's. And in 1962 on Mother's Day (which Flannery sarcastically called "the great commercial feast"), she presented Regina with a male burro named Ernest. "It was what she wanted," she told Maryat Lee about this unusual gift. And she added that they hoped to raise "little spotted mules."[38]

The plan to raise little mules worked. Ernest mated with Marquita, and a foal was born in September of 1963. In a letter to Hester, Flannery described the newborn as a long-legged black creature with a white mouth, about an eighth of the size of his mother. Perhaps referencing the time of year he was born, Regina named him Equinox, and Flannery added O'Connor. Proudly, she sent photos to Hester and to Janet McKane, who later sent Flannery a little china figurine of a burro as a keepsake.

Humpty Dumpty Field Trips

Mother and daughter might have enjoyed solitude and a rural life distant from the city, but they were far from hermits. They welcomed visitors to Andalusia, and invited schoolchildren to come and tour the grounds. Not surprisingly, Equinox proved especially fascinating to them.

Writing to McKane on November 5, 1963, Flannery explained that the routine was well-established: the children from Humpty Dumpty Kindergarten walked around the farm and looked at ponies, peacocks, swans, and ducks. Then they headed to Flannery's window. "I stick my head out, and the teacher says, 'And this is Miss Flannery. Miss Flannery is an author.'" The children went home, she added, "having seen a peacock and a donkey and a duck and a goose and an author."[39] What the children didn't realize, however, was that, every now and again, there were some unsavory creatures lurking around. One year, when the cub scouts and nursery school children were visiting, a farm hand killed a five-foot water rattler, but "no one was any the wiser."[40]

Ernest in the Manger

Apart from operating their own version of a children's zoo, each year, mother and daughter also provided animals to help local churches with their Christmas celebrations. "We're observing the season in an ecumenical way," Flannery told Father Romagosa early in December, 1963.[41] Apparently the three burros had been invited to appear in Christmas events in Milledgeville, but only Ernest, Equinox's father, was deemed tame enough to participate. He proved quite popular, showing up in the manger scene at the Hardwick Christian Church as well as in a pageant at a Methodist church. He did very well in the manger, but a snarl developed with the Methodists: "when the big moment came and the church [was] full of Methodists, he wouldn't put his foot inside the door." She concluded that he just didn't care for fellowship.[42]

Flannery was bedridden during what would be her last Christmas season, and too weak to attend Mass. Still, she took pleasure knowing the burros had participated in the local festivities. In the months to come, she was in and out of the hospital, and grew much weaker, but she continued to find delight and comfort in her animals. In April 1964 she wrote to a friend about the Muscovy duck laying eggs under the back steps. Also, the two new swans were conversing with each other, "while the peacocks scream and holler." In late June of 1964, she was growing very weak, but she still enjoyed looking out her window and reporting to friends what the animals were up to. "It is fine to be at home," she told McKane, mentioning that she was watching Equinox chasing the swans.[43]

✠   ✠   ✠   ✠

After Flannery's death, three pair of peafowl remained at Andalusia. One pair went to Stone Mountain, Georgia, and another to the sisters at Our Lady of Perpetual Help Home in Atlanta. The third pair took up residence at the Monastery of the Holy Spirit in rural Conyers. Within a year, however, the Stone Mountain birds met a violent end, becoming supper for predators. The pair at the cancer home eventually joined the birds at the monastery, and it was about two decades before they wore out their welcome there.[44]

Father Luke Kot, who still lives at the monastery, recalls that folks on retreat would be awakened by the birds at night: "The birds were beautiful, but they made strange noises, like someone being choked to death."[45] Flannery surely would have chuckled at this apt description. After all, she herself once had remarked that the birds sounded as though they were "being murdered slowly, repeatedly [and] formally."[46] Today, there are new peafowl at Andalusia, and it is heartening to note that Flossie, a descendant of the original burros, still makes her home on the farm. She was spotted recently, munching on some fine grasses near the barn and studiously ignoring visitors who were calling her name and waving at her.

Inside the farmhouse, on the mantle in Flannery's bedroom, a collection of items stands as quiet witness to her life. Sitting next to a crucifix is a framed black-and-white photo of a smiling Flannery in her college days. Nearby are a bottle of aspirin and a small statue of the

Madonna holding the Christ Child on her lap. Propped against the wall is one of Flannery's own color-pencil sketches of a peacock, and in front of that is the little china burro. If the crucifix was Flannery's reminder of the suffering at the heart of Christianity, and the Madonna a sign of her devotion to Mary (and perhaps of Regina's love for Flannery), then the jaunty little burro and the brightly colored peacock may have reminded her that when pain relievers fail, as they always do, Flannery could find respite from her ailments by contemplating the wonders of God's creation.

CHAPTER 12

Grace in Suffering: The Cross of Lupus

"Cheers" was Flannery's standard closing in her letters, even when she was bedridden. Even as she suffered – and, especially towards the end, the pain was terrible – she persevered in good humor. Her writing, her animals, and of course her friends, were sources of quiet joy in the midst of agony. Undoubtedly her faith, too, gave her strength and solace; however she had never expected Christianity to protect her from suffering. "What people don't realize is how much religion costs," she wrote. "They think faith is a big electric blanket, when of course it is the cross."[1]

Withholding the Truth

The first hint that something was wrong came in 1950, when twenty-five-year-old Flannery was living in a garage apartment behind the Fitzgeralds' house in rural Connecticut. Life there was pleasant, as she and her friends had settled into a comfortable routine: either Sally or Robert would drive with Flannery each morning to attend Mass at a church about four miles away, while the other stayed behind to watch the children and make breakfast. Later, in her small, bare-bones apartment, Flannery would work on her book for four hours, and then have lunch with the family. In the evenings, over martinis, she regaled Sally and Robert with funny stories about life in her home town, but also confided that she had no plans to live again in Georgia.

But then one day she casually mentioned a feeling of "heaviness" in her arms, which she thought was from typing. When the problem worsened, the Fitzgeralds took her to a doctor, who said it was probably arthritis and advised her to have a more thorough check-up when she went home for Christmas. On the train ride home she became desperately ill. When Flannery arrived, Regina rushed her to Baldwin County Hospital, where she was diagnosed with acute rheumatoid arthritis and then treated with cortisone. But the fevers and fatigue continued, and in January she was transferred to Emory Hospital in Atlanta, where she spent an entire month. The treatment included blood transfusions and then massive injections of a cortisone derivative. It was there that blood tests confirmed that she was suffering not from arthritis but from something far deadlier: lupus.

Lupus is an incurable disease that wreaks havoc on the body's immune system, causing it to attack healthy cells and tissues, resulting in damage to the joints, the skin, and organs. Symptoms include joint pain, swelling, fevers, rashes, hair loss, and fatigue. With the first attack, Flannery experienced severe swelling in her face and loss of hair due to the high fevers. "It is a fair indication of how sick she was," Robert Fitzgerald said, "that, until summer, we had no letter from her at all but corresponded through her mother."[2] When Flannery did finally go home from the hospital, she was too weak to climb the stairs at the Cline home in Milledgeville, so Regina decided to take her to the farm.

After the doctor warned Regina that her daughter might die, she and the rest of the family decided to withhold the truth from Flannery out of fear that full knowledge of her prognosis might somehow make her condition worsen. Thinking that she was suffering from rheumatoid arthritis, Flannery busied herself in the hospital with re-writing her novel *Wise Blood*. In any event, the treatment was harsh: She had to observe a completely salt-free diet and give herself daily injections. "It was all an ordeal," remarked Sally Fitzgerald, "but she believed that it was to be temporary."[3]

"Languishing on My Bed"

Once she was feeling well enough to write letters, Flannery downplayed her discomforts with her characteristic wit. Writing to a friend from the Baldwin Memorial "Horspital" two days before Christmas in 1950, she announced, "I am languishing on my bed of semi-affliction, this time with AWTHRITUS... what leaves you always willing to sit down." She added that she planned to remain in Milledgeville awhile, "waiting to see how much of an invalid I am going to get to be."[4] A few months later, she told a friend she was glad to be at home and was giving herself daily injections and doing "nothing that I can get out of doing."[5]

She had plenty to do, correcting proofs and revised galleys of *Wise Blood*, which was published in May of 1952. A month later, Flannery returned briefly to Connecticut to see the Fitzgeralds, smuggling three ducklings on the plane as gifts for their children. She stayed with them for five weeks, until a viral infection made her symptoms worsen and she returned home, where she had to spend six weeks in bed.

Graceful Acceptance

Perhaps her calm reaction to what she believed was a temporary bout of arthritis is not that startling. But in the summer of 1952, when Flannery learned the true nature of her illness, her faith really shone through. At that point, she realized that she would not be returning to her garage apartment in Connecticut, so she asked the Fitzgeralds to send her clothing and books to Milledgeville and then began adjusting to life at Andalusia. Sally Fitzgerald described Flannery's acceptance of the diagnosis as "graceful," rather than merely stoic.[6] In many ways, this description seems perfect, because it would indeed take generous outpourings of God's grace for Flannery to endure the suffering that was in store for her. As Fitzgerald noted, it helped that Flannery believed strongly in "passive diminishments" – Pierre Teilhard de Chardin's term to describe the acceptance of suffering that we cannot change.[7]

According to Robert Ellsberg, passive diminishment means that "our spiritual character is formed as much by what we endure and what is taken from us as it is by our achievements and our conscious choices."[8] In de Chardin's view, accepting ill fortune, whether it is disease, old age, or accident, is part of the journey to holiness.[9] In a letter to McKane, Flannery herself defined passive diminishments as "those afflictions that you can't get rid of and have to bear." Always level-headed, though, she also emphasized that de Chardin "believes you must bend every effort *to* get rid of" those afflictions that can be overcome or avoided.[10]

There was something else happening in her life at about the same time that she was dealing with lupus, and it might have brought her much happiness if only things had worked out. About a year after learning the true gravity of her condition, she met Erik Langkjaer, a Danish-born textbook salesman, who became a frequent guest at Andalusia. They dated for about a year, and Flannery fell in love with him, but it seems he did not return her feelings. When he decided to return to Denmark in 1954, she was quite distressed.[11] They wrote to each other after that, but in his last letter to her, he announced that he would be marrying someone else.[12]

Taking It All as a Blessing

Flannery kept many things to herself. She didn't write about this relationship in her letters – except for a brief mention to Hester, a few years later, of a fellow she used to "go with" – nor did she alarm her friends about her illness, or go out of her way to arouse their sympathy. Instead, she made jokes at her own expense. As the year 1953 opened, she reported to the Fitzgeralds that the medication's side effects had rendered her practically "bald-headed on top and [with] a watermelon face." Despite the disfigurements, and having to avoid sun and exercise, she insisted her situation was "no great hardship."[13] On St. Patrick's Day of the same year, she told her friends Elizabeth and Robert Lowell that lupus was "one of those things in the rheumatic department; it comes and goes. When it comes I retire and when it goes, I venture forth." On a hopeful note, she added that, in her father's day, "there was nothing for [the disease] but the undertaker," whereas she was able to control the illness with medication.[14]

For non-believers, Flannery's almost cheerful attitude might be hard to fathom. Suffering, pain, and illness are things to be scorned, hated, and run away from. Add to that a broken relationship, and many people might fall into despair. For this woman of faith, however, life existed on two levels. There was the ordinary, everyday world of writing stories, going to doctors, and feeding birds. But there was also the deeper, mystical realm, in which her life was a journey with Jesus Christ. True, that journey involved suffering, but she trusted Christ to give her the grace she needed to persevere. As she told the Lowells, "I can with one eye squinted take it all as a blessing."

Better to Pray Than Grieve

The "passive diminishments" from lupus were dark and burdensome. They started with a limp, first mentioned in a letter dated February 12, 1954, which the doctors initially thought was due to rheumatism. In her typical fashion, Flannery declared that it galled her to have lupus and then be stricken with mere rheumatism – a "vulgar disease at best"[15] – and described her gait as giving her the appearance of being a little drunk all the time. In November, she assured her mentor, Caroline Gordon Tate, that the limp didn't bother her.

Flannery refused to label her life a tragedy. She accepted the good and the bad with equanimity, because she accepted everything as the will of God. Her admiration for those who surrender to his will was expressed in a letter to a friend about her story "The Temple of the Holy Ghost," published in a magazine in 1954. She explained that she had based the hermaphrodite in the story on a real person she'd seen at a local fair who'd told the crowd that God had made him that way. For Flannery, the character of the hermaphrodite revealed a poignant resignation to suffering, which she described as one of the fruits of the Holy Ghost.[16]

Flannery also refused to succumb to self-pity. In a letter penned on New Year's Day, 1955, she emphasized that she did not see life as a tragedy, but rather as the will of God. She admitted that grief was an ordinary part of life, but said she was suspicious of her own grief because it so easily could become self-pity in "sheep's clothing." She went on to say that it is "better to pray than to grieve; and it is greater to be joyful than to grieve." And she added: "It takes more grace to be joyful than any but the greatest have."[17]

Practicing Self-Denial

Joy in the face of suffering might seem impossible to achieve, but to avoid gloominess Flannery relied on God's grace – a grace, she told one correspondent, that came through the sacraments.[18] Writing to T.R. Spivey, a Protestant, she acknowledged that many things that bring Catholics grace – going to Mass, regular fasting – are done out of obligation, or become "merely habit." However, she believed that it was better to "be held to the Church by habit than not to be held at all." What's more, she believed that by prescribing such habitual obligations, the Church showed itself to be "mighty realistic" about human nature, since obligations provide needed structure.[19] They also bring opportunities for grace.

Flannery believed there was something we can do to make ourselves more receptive to God's free gift of grace:

"You have to practice self-denial," she told Spivey.[20] For her that meant immersing herself in writing: "I never completely forget myself except when I am writing," she wrote to Hester.[21] She also practiced self-denial by giving money to charity rather than spending it on herself. Flannery had money to give only because, like a true monastic, she did not require much to live on – not because she had a great surplus of cash. The dairy farm provided the basics for Regina and Flannery, with book royalties adding a little extra to the coffers. And it was indeed only a little: at a time when paperback books sold for about twenty-five cents a copy, royalties from her fiction were modest at first. Fitzgerald mentions that Flannery earned a mere $1.35 from *Wise Blood* in its first six months, and $62.16 from selling the English serial rights to "A Temple of the Holy Ghost."

Although Flannery doesn't discuss money in detail in her letters, we do get a few glimpses. We know that she and Regina depended at times on the generosity of Cousin Katie and certainly would never have been able to afford the trip to Lourdes without her. We know Flannery wasn't that keen on public speaking, but the talks at various colleges earned her about $50 each time, and she continued on the circuit because the money helped pay the bills. In 1956, when she received a large sum of money – $800 – from the sale of a story to a television production company, Flannery used the money to buy Regina a new refrigerator.

She didn't spend money on clothing (Regina made her dresses), but she did enjoy ordering books; however, even here her frugality is evident, as she would often ask Hester to send her books checked out from the Atlanta Public Library. In 1959, when she was awarded an $8000 grant from the Ford Foundation, which was supposed to help her with her writing for two years, she told friends that she would stretch the money to last five times that long.

Still, when she was able to, Flannery gave generously and without condition. Once, she wrote to Father McCown telling him that she had made some extra money from a talk and wanted "to get rid of a little of it."[22] Enclosed was a check, and a suggestion that he use it "for the children."

The Mystery of Grace

"The action of grace changes a character," Flannery explained.[23] She was referring to fictional characters, but her remark holds true for real life also. We are given graces to endure what might seem unbearable to others. It is true that this spiritual gift is mysterious: we can't see it or measure it, any more than we can weigh love, but grace subtly works changes in the soul.

"Grace can't be experienced in itself," Flannery told Hester. She said that when you receive the Body and Blood of Christ, grace flows into your soul, "but you experience nothing; or if you do experience something, what you experience is not the grace but an emotion caused by it."

As an author, Flannery tried to portray grace through its effects on the characters in her stories. In "The Artificial Nigger," Mr. Head is changed as he stands before the broken and battered statue of the black man, "even though he remains Mr. Head." As she put it, he was not really "the same man at the end of the story."[24] These words help unlock the mystery of the author's own grace. Over the years, she remained Flannery O'Connor, but God's grace slowly was changing her, making her better able to bear suffering.

We see this occurring bit by bit in her letters, as she altered her dreams to accommodate her illness. She had told her friends she didn't want to live in Georgia, and looked forward to returning to her little apartment in Connecticut. She had at first thought her illness was temporary. Yet she accepted the more serious diagnosis; she sent for her books and her clothing so she could get on with her life at the farm. And as the disease began crippling her, she made the necessary adjustments with little complaint.

An Ape on Crutches

As walking became increasingly painful, by the end of 1954 Flannery began using a cane. Her hipbone continued to deteriorate, and in the fall of 1955, the cane gave way to crutches, which she hoped would be merely a temporary measure. "I feel like a large stiff anthropoid ape," she wrote to Hester.[25] The doctors told her that if she kept the weight off her hip for a year or two, the situation might improve. If not, "in my old age I will be charging people from my wheelchair."[26] To her friend Fanny Cheney, she declared that she'd told her mother to "take out insurance on me and all the people I trip and kill while I am on these things."[27]

Since she was not the sporty or outdoorsy type, she assured Hester, the crutches didn't inconvenience her much. "My greatest exertion and pleasure... has been throwing the garbage to the chickens and I can still do this, though I am in danger of going with it."[28] After a few months, the crutches began providing fodder for humorous tales. For example, she told Hester about an old lady on the elevator in Davison's department store in Atlanta who "fixed me with a moist gleaming eye and said in a loud voice, 'Bless you, darling!'" In return, Flannery shot her a "weakly lethal" look. This led the woman to whisper, "Remember what they said to John at the gate, darling!" Later, Flannery asked a one-legged friend about that biblical reference. "The lame shall enter first," the friend quoted. Flannery archly commented to Hester that this might be because the lame would use their crutches to knock everybody else aside.[29]

"Magnificent Fortitude"

On April 7, 1956, the doctors gave Flannery some bad news: "It's crutches for me from now on," she told Hester. "I will henceforth be a structure with flying buttresses."[30] A year later she wrote to Dawkins that the crutches meant she couldn't be active physically, so there was nothing left to do but write. "I may have a blessing in disguise." In a letter to Hester, Flannery revealed that this blessing included a chance to do what her father, also stricken young with lupus, could not. Writing made her extra happy, she said, because it was a fulfillment of her father's dream.[31]

As her symptoms worsened, one by one she informed her circle of friends. "You didn't know I had a DREAD DISEASE didja?" she wrote to Maryat Lee on February 11, 1958. She reported that her father had died of lupus at age forty-four, "but the scientists hope to keep me here until I am 96." Then she added, "I am bearing this with my usual magnificent fortitude."[32]

"A Place Where There's No Company"

Flannery typically accepted her suffering and slow decline with courage and humor, but after meeting Hester at Andalusia for the first time, in June of 1956, she did express some sorrow over her misfortune. Two things, she confessed to her friend, had changed her and made her feel isolated: sickness and success. "One of them alone wouldn't have done it for me but the combination was guaranteed."[33]

It's reasonable to think that newfound fame can alter old friendships, but for Flannery, it seems illness had made a bigger difference. "I have never been anywhere but sick," she said, and for her sickness was a place "more instructive than a long trip to Europe." Although her journey had yielded much self-knowledge, sickness for her was a lonely place, too. After all, only the suffering person can know the true extent of his pain; friends, no matter how compassionate, remain bystanders. "It's always a place where there's no company, where nobody can follow."[34]

One of God's Mercies

After these sorrowful admissions, the tone in this letter changed. Many people wish for a quick, painless death, Flannery continued, but she saw things differently. In fact, she believed that having a long, serious illness before death could bring a person closer to God. "Sickness before death is a very appropriate thing," she wrote, "and I think those who don't have it miss one of God's mercies."[35]

Many years later, Cardinal Joseph Ratzinger echoed her sentiment by asserting that those who suffer may enter into a sacramental fellowship with Christ. In *God and the World*, he wrote that, in a mystical way, illness can bring spiritual healing: "Christ, by teaching me how to suffer, and by suffering with me, may truly become my doctor, who overcomes the deep spiritual sickness within my soul."[36]

What's Your Bidnis?

By 1960, nearly ten years after the initial diagnosis, Flannery couldn't walk without crutches, and jaw pain made it hard for her to chew solid food. Nonetheless, she managed to maintain her matter-of-fact attitude toward her illness. On December 4, she told Father McCown she would be going into Piedmont Hospital to have her "bones inspected," because they were "melting or leaking or getting porous or something."[37] Four days later, she told Maryat Lee that her last X-rays were very bad. "It appears the jaw is going the same way the hip is." And she added, "I had noticed a marked change in the position of my mouth."[38]

Even in the hospital, Flannery was on the lookout for funny stories. On December 22, she reported to Hester that a sister from Our Lady of Perpetual Help Home had sent her "a box of cresants." An aunt had sent her six egg custards, but another friend outdid them all, contributing an artificial spider to frighten the nurses with.[39] Flannery also told Hester that the woman in admissions with "carrot-colored hair & eyeglasses to match" had asked her what she did for a living: "What's your bidnis?" When Flannery replied that she was a writer, the woman asked her to repeat the answer and then demanded, "How do you spell that?"[40]

Offering Up Difficult Hours

The results of the hospital tests were daunting: it seems that the steroid drugs she was taking to keep the disease under control were causing her bones to disintegrate. On Christmas Eve she told Hester that the doctors were going to stop the steroids. "Dr. M. says it is better to be alive with joint trouble than dead without it." She added, "Amen."[41]

On Christmas Day 1960, she wrote to Father Watson to tell him she would be embarking on a new course of treatment and asked for his prayers.[42] In his reply, the Jesuit priest assured her that he had been remembering her during daily Mass. He also made a request that would have struck a special chord with her: "Offer up one of your more difficult hours for a special intention of mine, and I shall hold myself deep in your debt."[43] Flannery, deeply mindful of the Catholic notion that suffering can be turned into good if we offer it to God for someone else's benefit, replied that she would remember his intention.[44]

Flannery still held out hope that she would eventually be able to walk without crutches. On June 23, 1961, she mentioned to Father McCown that, before summer was out, "I think I am going to have a steelhead put in my hip joint, thus eventually enabling me to get about on my own two feet." She asked him to pray that this was the Lord's will, and also for the success of the operation.[45] When the doctors ruled out the procedure as too dangerous, she accepted their decision calmly. Although she was no doubt very disappointed, in her next letter to Father McCown, she simply said, "Now I can forget about it."[46]

The Redemptive Experience of Joy

About a year before Flannery's death, McKane evidently had expressed to her a belief that suffering was a shared experience with Christ. In her reply, Flannery agreed, but she added an intriguing twist by noting that *every* experience, except sin, could be shared with Christ. Joy, for example, "may be a redemptive experience itself and not just the fruit of one."[47] This emphasis on joy probably would not have surprised Flannery's good friends, who were well aware of her abiding sense of humor and her ability to find hilarity in even the grimmest of circumstances.

Flannery's friend Thomas F. Gossett called her humor "uproarious and sometimes inward and ironic." It was Gossett who recorded for posterity a little known fact about Flannery, which is that she found many of her stories to be so funny that she could hardly control her laughter when reading them aloud. He recalled the day when Flannery had invited the students in his Southern Literature class to Andalusia to meet her, and they asked her to read "Good Country People," which features the atheist philosopher Hulga (formerly named Joy), and the young Bible salesman.

As Flannery read the story aloud, Gossett was surprised at "how deeply the humor of it affected her." Although many people might consider the seduction scene quite tragic (recall that the salesman leaves Hulga in the hayloft and absconds with her wooden leg), Flannery found the scene comical, especially the young man's parting comment: "I'll tell you another thing, Hulga... you ain't so smart. I been believing in nothing ever since I was born!" It was at this point that Flannery became so overcome by laughter that the book fell from her hands and hit the floor.

Gossett postulates that humor was such an inherent part of Flannery's personality that she might have unintentionally misled some of her friends in the last year of her life. He believes that she probably knew the seriousness of her condition, but her humorous comments sidetracked her friends from recognizing it. Where did that humor spring from? "Faith in the Christian religion," Gossett said simply.[48] Although he does not expand on this, it is clear that for the Christian, the sorrow of the Crucifixion cannot be separated from the joy of the Resurrection: these are inherent parts of our redemption.

Underpinning the redemption is the fact of the Incarnation itself: God walked among men and experienced not only human suffering but human joys. Flannery could see, then, how redemption and joy are thus inextricably bound together, not only theologically but also in everyday life. The joyful experience of, say, a peacock opening its tail, or a swan perched in a bird bath, can shake us out of our sorrow and redeem us from our worries.

Thérèse and the Cross

This same interweaving of joy and suffering brings to mind the saint whom Flannery so greatly admired: Thérèse of Lisieux was known to be a cheerful soul, despite the tragedies in her short life. She was only four when her mother died, and she suffered another sharp blow five years later when her older sister, Pauline, left home to enter the convent. Pauline had become a second mother for Thérèse, and the child's grief at losing her was so great that she became ill and bedridden for months.

But perhaps the greatest emotional distress for Thérèse came shortly after she herself had entered the convent and her father suffered a debilitating stroke from which he never fully recovered. It wasn't long after that her physical decline from tuberculosis began. Through it all, though, Thérèse clung to her belief that her suffering was a share in Christ's Cross, and her goal in the convent was to save souls. "As Jesus had told me he would give me souls through the Cross," she wrote in her autobiography, "I welcomed the Cross and my love of suffering grew steadily."[49] Thérèse was, however, quite human, and there were times when she complained, and times when she cried, but for her what counted most was her private intention, her unspoken desire to unite her sufferings with Jesus.

Flannery also was very aware of the Catholic belief in the redemptive quality of suffering, of offering our trials to God as a prayer to help others. Like Thérèse, she believed that everything was God's will, including the personal crosses we bear. As Thérèse so beautifully expressed it:

Everything is a grace, everything is the direct effect of our Father's love, difficulties, contradictions, humiliations, all the soul's miseries, her burdens, her needs, everything, because through them, she learns humility, realizes her weakness. Everything is a grace because everything is God's gift. Whatever be the character of life or its unexpected events – to the heart that loves, all is well.[50]

Although Flannery does not mention it in her letters, found among her possessions after her death was a small volume called *The Little Flower Prayer Book*. It contains the Carmelite devotions that Thérèse had relied on when she was in the convent, along with devotions to the saint and prayers written by her. In the litany of Saint Thérèse in this book, she is described as "cheerful in sacrifices, joyful in suffering, and the saint of childlike simplicity."

In the prayers composed by Thérèse herself, prayers that Flannery must have turned to in her final years, there is one passage that stands out: "I thank thee, O my God, for all the graces Thou hast granted me: especially for having purified me in the crucible of suffering." But we must keep in mind that Flannery most admired Thérèse because the saint seemed to be aware of her own very human failings, and she was far from sanctimonious. A keen glimmer of this self-knowledge is shown in a prayer written by Thérèse in which she asked for the grace to be humble, and acknowledges to God what she considered her greatest weakness: pride.[51]

Laughing Virgin and Child

The rooms of Flannery's home at Andalusia contained crucifixes; there was a framed print on the stairway wall of the Sacred Heart of Jesus, and another upstairs of "After Golgotha," showing the weeping figure of Mary with the cross in the distance. Many Catholic homes have similar reminders of Christ's passion – crucifixes, holy cards, and religious paintings – but Flannery had an interest in something that was much more difficult to come by. And on June 5, 1963, about a year before her death, she wrote to her Catholic friend McKane, to ask her help in finding a certain statue of the Madonna and Child that she had seen on a 1949 visit to the Cloisters in the Metropolitan Museum of Art in New York City. There are, of course, countless artistic renderings of the Blessed Virgin Mary and the baby Jesus, but Flannery had noticed a particular joyful quality about this one that attracted her.

I particularly remember one statue that I saw there. It was the Virgin holding the Christ child and both were laughing... I've never seen any models of it anywhere but I was greatly taken with it and should I ever get back to the Cloisters, which is unlikely, I mean to see if it is there.[52]

She asked McKane if the statue sounded familiar, which must have prompted the schoolteacher to do some homework. Before long, she sent Flannery a large photograph of the smiling Virgin and Child,[53] which she'd evidently obtained from the museum. It's most likely an early fourteenth-century statue from France called simply, "Virgin and Child, Seated" and located in the Cloisters 1925 collection.

"Commend Me to the Lord"

It is little wonder that Flannery was delighted by the photograph of the smiling Madonna and child, as she was also the one who had praised the biography of St. Thérèse that showed her human flaws rather than portraying her as impossibly pious and holy. We can imagine Flannery tucking the photograph away, perhaps in her *Little Flower Prayer Book* or breviary. She might have turned to the prayers – and the smiling face of the Madonna – more and more as additional health problems stalked her. For if lupus wasn't bad enough, she was also battling anemia, caused by a fibroid tumor. It seems that her red-blood-cell count was so low that she recently had fainted, but in a letter written to Hester on Christmas Day, 1963, Flannery made light of her affliction: "Not enough blood to run the engine or something."[54] Bedridden and weak, she told McKane on New Year's Eve that she had missed Mass on Christmas. She even lacked sufficient energy to use an electric typewriter. [55]

Her internist was reluctant to allow surgery on a lupus patient, but the situation was becoming dire, so he scheduled an operation to remove the tumor on February 25, 1964. She noted to friends that it was all "fairly sudden." Five days before the surgery, she dropped the usual joking tone in a letter written to Father McCown: "Rather serious, so kindly commend me to the Lord, formally and informally."[56]

"Last Battle to Live"

A few weeks later, Flannery wrote to Robert Fitzgerald declaring the surgery a "howling success," and saying she would soon be restored by eating "potlicker," a Southern-style soup made with turnip greens. Sadly, things weren't that simple. The good news was that the tumor was not malignant, but Flannery was soon battling the after-effects of surgery, which included cystitis and a kidney infection.[57] According to Sally Fitzgerald, as the infections continued and a series of antibiotics proved fruitless in treating them, Flannery's "last battle to live" had begun, and although she may have suspected the end was near, her main concern was to complete her next collection of stories.[58]

The Heavy Wood of the Cross

As ever, Flannery was not alone in her struggle. Friends did their part by praying for her, and those who were priests celebrated Masses in her name. Father Watson, who was grieving the recent death of his brother, penned her a beautiful, comforting letter. "You are too wise and experienced in suffering for me to offer you any facile 'explanation' of the *mystery* of pain," he wrote on March 12, 1964. The kind priest went on to remind her of "the hope of heaven and the fact of God's love," and assured her that she was not carrying her cross alone: "I know that your spirit is strong (because your faith is great) and I wanted you to realize that now, better than before, I can feel with you, and thus perhaps in some little way help you bear the rough, heavy wood of your own cross."[59]

In her last letter to him, written three days later, Flannery expressed sympathy about his brother's death:

"I know the pain of a loss like that's greater than any kind of physical pain." She also reported that she had come through "very well" from the operation, but had not regained her strength. "I guess that will come back in time." Ever mindful of her writing vocation, she added, "Then I will just pray to have something to write that will be worth the expense of energy." Thanking Father Watson for his prayers, she promised to pray for him and for the repose of his brother's soul.[60]

Creaking Along to Age 96

Flannery continued battling numerous infections in the months following surgery, returning to the hospital in late March and then being confined to bed after her release in early April. On April 2, 1964, she told McKane that the doctors had tried five different antibiotics on her kidney infection, without success. Unfortunately, the medicines had wreaked havoc on her stomach and swollen her eyes shut.[61] She admitted to Father McCown that she would not be "out of the woods" for a few months, since there was a concern that the stress from surgery might reactivate her lupus. But in a letter to Maryat Lee she resumed the down-home Southern persona that characterized their correspondence, declaring herself optimistic, since her family was full of people who "creaked along" to about the age of 96. "Look for me to be this kind too."[62]

Another letter, however, reveals her deeper worry. Concerned about her next collection of stories, Flannery wrote in early May to her agent, Elizabeth McKee, telling her that she would be out of commission for the summer and "maybe longer." Since she was bedridden and could not type, she asked McKee if the collection could be put together using stories that had been published in magazines. This would eliminate the process of rewriting them, which she was not up to physically. However, she later decided to try to complete two unfinished stories, "Judgment Day" and "Parker's Back," to be included in this collection.

Last Letters

On May 21, 1964, Flannery was back in Piedmont Hospital in Atlanta with the two unfinished stories hidden under her pillow, since she feared that the doctors would forbid her to work on them. She had just signed a contract for what would be her last collection of stories, selecting the name *Everything That Rises Must Converge,* and she was eager to complete the last two stories.

But by early June, Flannery seemed discouraged about her health. "I don't know if I'm making progress or if there is any to be made," she told Lee.[63] Writing to Hester two days later, she confessed, "It sure don't look like I'll ever get out of this joint."[64] When Sessions saw her for the last time, it was in June and in the hospital. Her voice was strong, he noted, "but her body had more bruises and skin rashes" than he had ever remembered. Still, despite her ravaged appearance, it was her humor that struck him, "more in her piercing eyes than in her voice," a humor that "charged and volleyed and embraced as always." He added plaintively, "If I had known, I would not have believed that she was dying."[65]

It must have been a huge relief for Flannery when on June 20 she was allowed to leave the hospital and return home. The doctors put her on a diet that restricted her intake of proteins, so her kidneys would not be overtaxed. They also ordered her to remain in bed and take it easy. Under the watchful eye of Regina, she followed the doctors' orders, resting in bed most of the day and making changes to her stories in longhand. About a week later, she was able to do a little work at the electric typewriter, and continued revising stories for the new collection. On July 7 when a priest visited to bring her Holy Communion, by her request she also received what she referred to as the "now-called Sacrament of the Sick," traditionally given to the dying and known as Extreme Unction.[66]

Flannery was not home long. By the end of July, she was back in Baldwin County Hospital with a kidney infection. On July 25, in her very last letter to Hester, she shared the good news about her story "Revelation," which had won first prize in the O. Henry Awards. She also said that she'd received another blood transfusion, with little effect. Writing to McKane for the last time on July 27, she thanked her for sending a china figurine of a burro that reminded Flannery of Equinox, one of the burros at Andalusia.

Flannery wrote her very last letter, to Maryat Lee, on July 28, 1964, six days before her death. It was written in a nearly illegible scrawl and found on Flannery's bedside table after her death. It seems that Lee had received an upsetting anonymous phone call. Characteristically concerned for others before herself, Flannery advised her friend to "be properly scared" and call the police. She closed with words revealing her abiding desire to get back to her vocation – "Don't know when I'll send those stories. I've felt too bad to type them" – and signed off her last written work with her usual "Cheers."[67]

Uniquely Practicing Charity

Flannery died of kidney failure on August 3, 1964. She was thirty-nine. The next day, Monsignor Joseph G. Cassidy, pastor of the Cathedral of Christ the King in Atlanta, celebrated a Requiem Mass at Sacred Heart Church in Milledgeville. She was buried in that town, beside her father's grave at Memory Hill cemetery. The tombstone is plain with just her parents' names, her name, and the necessary dates, but there also is a simple cross and the letters "IHS" – a traditional Christogram taken from the Greek name for Jesus – engraved in the marble.

On August 6, Atlanta Archbishop Paul J. Hallinan, who had visited Andalusia in 1962 and earned Flannery's great admiration, penned a column in *The Georgia Bulletin* about the community's loss. "Death has taken a fellow Georgian, a woman of charm, an artist with an authentic grasp of the South," he wrote. He praised her as a writer who served "the cause of the supernatural by a working knowledge of the secular," and noted that society tends to think of nurses, mothers, and social workers as performers of acts of mercy; however, he believed that those who write, sing, and draw may also practice charity in a unique way. "Our South and our Church are poorer because of the death of this fine young writer," he wrote. "But we are confident that the Judgment decrees include the artist as well as the mother, the nurse, the worker in social needs."[68] He then quoted Jesus Christ: "Whatever you did for the least of these, you did for Me."

Preparing for Death in Christ

A few months before her death, Flannery had said to Father Romagosa, "I've got pieces of a novel in the back of my head…. I figure it all comes in its own good time and I'm not going to worry about it."[69] Had she lived longer, there surely would have been many more novels, many more short stories. Had Flannery been writing the story of her life, however, it's doubtful that she would have characterized the ending as tragic. "It all comes in its own good time" are the words of a woman who knows that she is not in full control of her fate. They are the words of the same woman who had written in *A Memoir of Mary Ann* that the "creative action of the Christian's life was to prepare his death in Christ."

She believed that life was a journey to God, and she made the trip in a unique and enjoyable fashion. She loved her life at Andalusia, reveled in her friendships, and delighted in her birds. She also insisted that she didn't lead a holy life, but those who knew her well recognized her inner grace. Father McCown called her the most honest person he ever knew. And Sister Evangelist had declared that Flannery was a very saintly person.

✠   ✠   ✠   ✠

There are some today who hope that Flannery O'Connor will follow in Thérèse's footsteps and one day become not only a saint, but a doctor of the Church, largely based on her defense of the Faith in her letters. Flannery might flinch at the very mention of such a possibility – but so did Thérèse, who admitted in her autobiography that although she had always wanted to become a saint, "when I have compared myself with the saints, I have always found that there is the same difference between the saints and me as there is between a mountain whose summit is lost in the clouds and a humble grain of sand trodden underfoot by passers-by." Despite this notion, she refused to be discouraged, since she figured her longing came from God. She decided she would still aim at becoming a saint and would learn to put up with herself and her "countless faults."[70]

Flannery may one day be declared a saint, but I think she would be quick to say that she'd never want to see her touched-up, Technicolor face in some sweet children's prayer book, or to be smothered in plaster roses like poor St. Thérèse. If Flannery is declared a saint, then let her be a saint seen standing on the steps of Anadalusia, leaning on her crutches with a peacock brandishing his finery in front of her and a duck at her side. If she is declared a saint, then let her be a saint sitting next to Regina in the pew at Sacred Heart church, blanching at the St. Patrick's Day decorations. Let her be a saint gazing with equal parts piety and irony at the pilgrims of Lourdes, dreading the moment of bathing in the grotto. Let her be a saint who laughs so loud that books fall from her hands. Let her be a saint from whose pen stampede the wild-eyed Hazel Motes, the lumbering Hulga, the dazed Mrs. Turpin. Let her be a saint in the same way that Thérèse was – in her own "human and terrible greatness."

Prayer to Saint Raphael the Archangel

O Raphael, lead us toward those we are waiting for, those who are waiting for us:

Raphael, Angel of happy meetings, lead us by the hand toward those we are looking for. May all our movements be guided by your Light and transfigured with your Joy.

Angel, guide of Tobias, lay the request we now address to you at the feet of Him on whose unveiled Face you are privileged to gaze.

Lonely and tired, crushed by the separations and sorrows of life, we feel the need of calling you and of pleading for the protection of your wings, so that we may not be as strangers in the province of joy, all ignorant of the concerns of our country.

Remember the weak, you who are strong, you whose home lies beyond the region of thunder, in a land that is always peaceful, always serene and bright with the resplendent glory of God.

About the Author

Lorraine V. Murray is the author of *Grace Notes, Why Me? Why Now?*, *Confessions of an Ex-Feminist*, and a mystery novel, *Death in the Choir*. She's also a columnist with the *Atlanta Journal-Constitution* and the *Georgia Bulletin*, and works part-time at the Pitts Theology Library at Emory University. Lorraine and her husband, Jef, live in Decatur, Georgia, and are parishioners at St. Thomas More Catholic Church. Her website is www.lorrainevmurray.com.

Bibliography

Amason, Craig R. Interview, Andalusia Farm, Milledgeville, Georgia, June 8, 2007.

_____. E-mail interviews: March 3, May 7, May 9, May 22, and June 1, 2009.

Andalusia Farm Web site: www.andalusiafarm.org

"Author's Beloved Peacocks Come to Violent End." *The Post and Courier,* Charleston, South Carolina, November 29, 1991, 10-B.

Baltimore Catechism No. 3 Prepared and Enjoined by Order of the Third Plenary Council of Baltimore. Rockford, Illinois: Tan Books and Publishers, 1974.

Baumgaertner, Jill P. *A Proper Scaring.* Chicago: Cornerstone Press, 1999.

Bro, Bernard. *The Little Way: The Spirituality of Thérèse of Lisieux.* London: Darton, Lonman, and Todd, Ltd., 1997.

Carol, Angela. *St. Raphael.* Rockford, Illinois: Tan Books and Publishers, Inc., 1999.

Cash, Jean W. *Flannery O'Connor: A Life.* Knoxville: University of Tennessee Press, 2002.

Catholic Church. *The Catechism of the Catholic Church.* Vatican City: Libreria Editrice Vaticana, 1994.

Combes, André. *The Spirituality of St. Thérèse: An Introduction.* New York: P. J. Kenedy and Sons, 1950.

Crabtree, Chaminade, O.C.S.O, Letter to author, July 13, 2007.

Dominican Nuns of Our Lady of Perpetual Help Home, Atlanta, Georgia. *A Memoir of Mary Ann.* New York: Dell Publishing Company, 1962. (paperback edition).

_____. *A Memoir of Mary Ann.* Savannah: Frederic C. Beil, 1991. (hardback edition).

Dominican Sisters of Hawthorne Web Site: http://www.hawthorne-dominicans.org/

Downey, Columba, editor. *The Little Flower Prayer Book: A Carmelite Manual of Prayer.* Chicago: Carmelite Press, 1926.

Elie, Paul. *The Life You Save May Be Your Own: An American Pilgrimage.* New York: Farrar, Straus, and Giroux, 2003.

Ellsberg, Robert. *Flannery O'Connor: Spiritual Writings.* Maryknoll, New York: Orbis Books, 2003.

_____. *The Saints' Guide to Happiness.* New York: Doubleday, 2003.

Emerson, Bo. "Mystery Begins to Unravel," *The Atlanta Journal-Constitution*, March 1, 2009, H12.

Enniss, Stephen. E-mail interview, May 25, 2007.

Farmer, David. *The Oxford Dictionary of Saints*, 4th ed. Oxford: Oxford University Press, 1997.

Fitzgerald, Robert. Introduction to *Everything That Rises Must Converge* by Flannery O'Connor. New York: Farrar, Straus, and Giroux, 1965.

Fitzgerald, Sally. "Chronology" in *Collected Works* by Flannery O'Connor. New York: Library of America, 1988.

The Georgia Bulletin. "Flannery O'Connor Dead," August 6, 1964.

Giannone, Richard. Introduction to *Flannery O'Connor: Spiritual Writings* by Robert Ellsberg. Maryknoll, New York: Orbis Books, 2003.

Gordon, Sarah and Craig Amason. *A Literary Guide to Flannery O'Connor's Georgia.* Athens: University of Georgia Press, 2008.

Gossett, Thomas F. "Flannery O'Connor's Humor with a Serious Purpose." *Studies in American Humor*, Volume 3, Number 3, January 1977, 174–179.

Hallinan, Paul J. "Archbishop's Notebook." *The Georgia Bulletin*, August 6, 1964, Vertical File, Special Collections, Georgia College and State University Library and Instructional Technology Center, Milledgeville, Georgia.

Holden, Anne Marie, O.P. Letter to author, July 11, 2007.

Keiser, Gretchen. "Cancer Home Sisters Celebrate 50 Years of Service." *The Georgia Bulletin*, April 20, 1989.

Kilcourse, George A., Jr. *Flannery O'Connor's Religious Imagination: A World with Everything Off Balance.* Mahwah, New Jersey: Paulist Press, 2001.

Kot, Luke, O.C.S.O. Phone interview, June 27, 2007.

Kreeft, Peter. *The Philosophy of Jesus.* South Bend, Indiana: Saint Augustine's Press, 2007.

Lewis, C. S. *Mere Christianity: The Case for Christianity, Christian Behavior, and Beyond Personality.* Westwood, New Jersey: Barbour and Company, Inc., 1985.

Lyden, Jacki. Interview with Stephen Enniss. National Public Radio, "All Things Considered," May 12, 2007.

Martin, Regis. *Flannery O'Connor: Unmasking the Devil.* Ann Arbor, Michigan: Sapientia Press, 2005.

May, John R., ed. "Blue-Bleak Embers: The Letters of Flannery O'Connor and Youree Watson," *The New Orleans Review*, 6.4 (1979): 336–356.

McCown, James Hart, S. J. Letters to Flannery O'Connor, The Thomas F. Gossett Collection, Rare Book, Manuscripts, and Special Collections Library, Duke University, Durham, North Carolina.

———. *With Crooked Lines: Early Years of an Alabama Jesuit*. Mobile, Alabama: Spring Hill College Press, 1990.

———. "Remembering Flannery O'Connor." *America*, September 8, 1979, 86–88.

Merton, Thomas. "Flannery O'Connor: A Prose Elegy" in *Raids on the Unspeakable*. New York: New Directions Books, 1966.

Monks of St. John's Abbey, eds. *A Short Breviary for Religious and the Laity*, 4th ed. Liturgical Press: Collegeville, Minnesota, 1949.

Mullen, Mary de Paul, O.P. E-mail to author, September 6, 2007.

Mullins, C. Ross, Jr. "Flannery O'Connor: An Interview." In *Conversations with Flannery O'Connor*, ed. Rosemary M. Magee. Jackson: University Press of Mississippi, 1987.

O'Connor, Flannery. *Collected Works*. Selected and edited by Sally Fitzgerald. New York: The Library of America, 1988.

———. *The Habit of Being: Letters of Flannery O'Connor*. Selected and edited by Sally Fitzgerald. New York: Farrar, Straus, and Giroux, 1979.

———. Introduction to *A Memoir of Mary Ann*. Dominican Nuns of Our Lady of Perpetual Help Home, Atlanta, Georgia. Savannah: Frederic C. Beil, 1991.

———. *Last Will and Testament of Mary Flannery O'Connor*, April 18, 1958. Vertical File, Special Collections, Georgia College and State University Library and Instructional Technology Center, Milledgeville, Georgia.

———. Letters to Betty Hester. Manuscripts, Archives, and Rare Book Library, Emory University, Atlanta, Georgia.

———. Letters to Father J.H. McCown. Thomas F. Gossett Papers, Rare Book, Manuscript, and Special Collections Library, Duke University, Durham, North Carolina.

———. Letters to Sister Julie. Sally Fitzgerald Papers, Manuscript, Archives, and Rare Book Library, Emory University, Atlanta, Georgia.

———, Letters to Sister Mary Evangelist Daly, O.P. Archives, Dominican Sisters of Hawthorne, Rosary Hill Home, Hawthorne, New York.

———. Letter to Sister Mary Josephine Lynaugh, O.P. Archives, Dominican Sisters of Hawthorne, Rosary Hill Home, Hawthorne, New York.

———. *Mystery and Manners: Occasional Prose*. Selected and edited by Sally and Robert Fitzgerald. New York: Farrar, Straus, and Giroux, 1970.

Our Lady of Perpetual Help Home Web site: http://www.olphhome.org/

Pridgen, Allen. *Walker Percy's Sacramental Landscapes: The Search in the Desert*. Selinsgrove: Susquehanna University Press, 2000.

Rath, Sura P. "An Evolving Friendship: Flannery O'Connor's Correspondence with Father Edward J. Romagosa, S. J." *Flannery O'Connor Bulletin*, 17 (1988–1989): 1–10.

Ratzinger, Joseph Cardinal. *God and the World: Believing and Living in Our Time.* San Francisco: Ignatius Press, 2002.

Robo, Etienne. *Two Portraits of St. Teresa of Lisieux.* Westminster, Maryland: Newman Press, 1957.

Romagosa, Edward J. Letter to author, undated, postmarked July 12, 2007.

Russell, Kenneth C. "St. Therese of Lisieux on Suffering." *Spiritual Life: A Journal of Contemporary Spirituality*, Volume 46, Number 4, Winter 2000, 230–238.

Scott, David. *A Revolution of Love: The Meaning of Mother Teresa.* Chicago: Loyola Press, 2005.

Sessions, William A. E-mail interviews: January 7, March 5, May 12, 2009.

_____. "Betty Hester: A Noble Soul." http://www2.gcsu.edu/library/sc/collections/oconnor/hester.html

_____, "Flannery O'Connor: A Memoir," *National Catholic Reporter*, October 28, 1964, Volume 1, Issue 1, page 9.

St. Joseph Daily Missal ed. Rev. Hugo H. Hoever. Great Falls, Montana: St. Bonaventure Publications, 2004.

Stephens, C. Ralph, ed. *The Correspondence of Flannery O'Connor and the Brainard Cheneys.* Jackson: University Press of Mississippi, 1986.

Tagami, Kirsten. "Women of Letters," *Atlanta Journal-Constitution*, May 10, 2007, A1, A16.

Thérèse of Lisieux. *The Autobiography of Saint Thérèse of Lisieux: The Story of a Soul.* Translated by John Beevers. New York: Doubleday, 1989.

Uhler, Margaret A. and Dorris P. Neligan. "One Hundred Years of Sacred Heart Catholic Church 1874-1974." Vertical File, Special Collections, Georgia College and State University Library and Instructional Technology Center, Milledgeville, Georgia.

Wawrykow, Joseph P. *The Westminster Handbook to Thomas Aquinas.* Louisville, Kentucky: Westminster John Knox Press, 2005.

Wood, Ralph C. *Flannery O'Connor and the Christ-Haunted South.* Grand Rapids, Michigan: Wm. B. Eerdmans Publishing Company, 2004.

_____. "Such a Catholic," *National Review*, March 9, 2009, Volume 61, Issue 4, 38–42.

Zuber, Leo J. and Carter W. Martin, Editors. *The Presence of Grace and Other Book Reviews by Flannery O'Connor.* Athens: University of Georgia Press, 1983.

NOTES

Preface and Introduction

1. Maurice Baring, *Darby and Joan*, Leipzig: Bernhard Tauchnitz, 1936, pp. 156-7
2. Quoted in D.M. Thomas, *Solzhenitsyn: A Century in His Life*, London: Little, Brown and Company, 1998, p. 194
3. Natalya Reshetovskaya, *Sanya: My Life with Alexander Solzhenitsyn*, Indianapolis/New York: Bobbs-Merrill Company, Inc., 1975, p. 115
4. Quoted in D.M. Thomas, *Solzhenitsyn: A Century in His Life*, London: Little, Brown and Company, 1998, p. 194
5. Pearce, *Solzhenitsyn: A Soul in Exile*, p. 308
6. Regis Martin, *Unmasking the Devil: Dramas of Sin and Grace in the World of Flannery O'Connor*, Ypsilanti, Michigan: Sapientia Press, 2002
7. Flannery O'Connor, *Mystery and Manners: Occasional Prose*, New York: Farrar, Straus and Giroux, 1974, p. 118
8. Fyodor Dostoyevsky, *The Brothers Karamazov*, Spark Educational Publishing (Barnes & Noble Classics), 2004, p. 107
9. O'Connor, *Mystery and Manners*, p. 173
10. Ibid., p.118
11. James H. McCown, "Remembering Flannery O'Connor," *America*, September 8, 1979, 87
12. Richard Giannone in Robert Ellsberg, *Flannery O'Connor: Spiritual Writings* (Maryknoll, New York: Orbis Books, 2003), 23
13. Flannery O'Connor, *The Habit of Being: Letters of Flannery O'Connor,* selected and edited by Sally Fitzgerald (New York: Farrar, Straus, and Giroux, 1979), 422 (Note: Future references to this source will be noted as HB.)
14. HB, 209
15. HB, 230

16. HB, 227
17. HB, xi
18. HB, 342
19. Flannery O'Connor, *Collected Works,* selected and edited by Sally Fitzgerald (New York: The Library of America, 1988), 929
20. Sally Fitzgerald, "Chronology" in *Collected Works,* 1237
21. HB, 520
22. Margaret A. Uhler and Dorris P. Neligan, "One Hundred Years of Sacred Heart Catholic Church 1874–1974," O'Connor vertical file, Special Collections, Georgia College and State University Library and Instructional Technology Center, Milledgeville, Georgia, 2
23. Sally Fitzgerald, *Collected Works,* op.cit., 1237
24. HB, 142
25. Jean W. Cash, *Flannery O'Connor: A Life* (Knoxville: University of Tennessee Press, 2002), 15
26. Sally Fitzgerald, *Collected Works,* op. cit., 1238
27. Ibid., 1239
28. Ibid
29. Ibid., 1242–43
30. HB, 22
31. HB, 514
32. HB, 290–91
33. HB, 288
34. Flannery O'Connor, Letter to Betty Hester, March 24, 1962, Manuscripts, Archives, and Rare Book Library, Emory University, Atlanta, Georgia
35. HB, 289
36. Flannery O'Connor, *Collected Works,* op. cit., 1075
37. C. Ralph Stephens, ed., *The Correspondence of Flannery O'Connor and the Brainard Cheneys* (Jackson: University Press of Mississippi, 1986), 71
38. Ibid., 52
39. HB, 114
40. Ralph C. Wood, "Such a Catholic," *National Review*, March 9, 2009: 38

Chapter 1

1. George A. Kilcourse, Jr., *Flannery O'Connor's Religious Imagination. A World with Everything Off Balance* (Mahwah, New Jersey: Paulist Press, 2001), 2
2. HB, 308
3. HB, 131
4. HB, 132
5. Ibid.
6. HB, 592
7. Ibid.

8. HB, 593
9. Ibid.
10. HB, 592
11. Regis Martin, *Flannery O'Connor: Unmasking the Devil* (Ann Arbor, Michigan: Sapientia Press, 2005), 61
12. HB, 456
13. Flannery O'Connor, "Evidence of Satan in Modern World" in Leo J. Zuber and Carter W. Martin, eds., *The Presence of Grace and Other Book Reviews by Flannery O'Connor* (Athens: University of Georgia Press: 1983), 139
14. HB, 367
15. HB, 360
16. HB, 367
17. HB, 361
18. *Saint Joseph's Daily Missal* (Great Falls, Montana: Saint Bonaventure Publications, 2004), 578
19. HB, 145
20. HB, 346
21. Flannery O'Connor, "A Temple of the Holy Ghost," *Collected Works*, op.cit., 208
22. HB, 159
23. HB, 161
24. HB, 521
25. Monks of St. John's Abbey, eds., A *Short Breviary for Religious and the Laity* (Collegeville, Minnesota: Liturgical Press, 1949), viii
26. Ibid., 65
27. Ibid., 21
28. Ibid., 66
29. Ibid., 97
30. Ibid., 129
31. Ibid., 159
32. Ibid., 222
33. Ibid., 26–27
34. Ibid., 48
35. Ibid., 43
36. HB, 310
37. HB, 468
38. HB, 480
39. HB, 518
40. HB, 483
41. HB, 498
42. HB, 572
43. HB, 582
44. Flannery O'Connor, Last Will and Testament of Mary Flannery O'Connor, April 18, 1958, O'Connor Vertical File, Special

Collections, Georgia College and State University Library and Instructional Technology Center, Milledgeville, Georgia

Chapter 2

1. Peter Kreeft, *The Philosophy of Jesus* (South Bend, Indiana: Saint Augustine's Press, 2007), 31
2. HB, 173
3. Flannery O'Connor, Letter to Father McCown, March 11, 1962, Thomas F. Gossett Papers, Duke University, Rare Book, Manuscript, and Special Collections Library, Durham, North Carolina
4. Flannery O'Connor, Letter to Father McCown, May 24, 1959, Thomas F. Gossett Papers, Duke University, Rare Book, Manuscript, and Special Collections Library, Durham, North Carolina
5. Bernard Bro, *The Little Way: The Spirituality of Therese of Lisieux* (London: Darton, Lonman, and Todd, Ltd.: 1997), 18
6. Ibid., 24–25
7. Ibid., 34
8. Ibid., 35
9. Paul Elie, *The Life You Save May Be Your Own: An American Pilgrimage* (New York: Farrar, Straus, and Giroux, 2003), 282
10. HB, 92
11. HB, 135
12. Leo Zuber and Martin, Carter, W., eds., *The Presence of Grace and Other Book Reviews by Flannery O'Connor* (Athens: University of Georgia Press, 1983), 19
13. HB, 135
14. Leo Zuber and Martin, Carter, op.cit., 18
15. HB, 516
16. Etienne Robo, *Two Portraits of St. Teresa of Lisieux* (Westminster, Maryland: Newman Press, 1957), 11
17. HB, 129
18. Ibid.
19. HB, 286
20. HB, 112
21. HB, 94
22. HB, 97
23. HB, 157. (The name of the novel is contained in the unedited version of this letter, which is stored in the Thomas F. Gossett Papers at Duke University.)
24. Joseph P. Wawrykow, *The Westminster Handbook to Thomas Aquinas* (Louisville, Kentucky: Westminster John Knox Press, 2005), 64
25. HB, 367
26. HB, 373

27. Flannery O'Connor, "On Her Own Work" in *Mystery and Manners* (New York: Farrar, Straus, and Giroux, 1970), 110

28. Ibid., 112

29. Flannery O'Connor, "Catholic Novelists" in *Mystery and Manners*, op. cit., 185

Chapter 3

1. HB, 90

2. HB, 134

3. Ibid.

4. HB, 93

5. Ibid.

6. HB, 92

7. C. S. Lewis, *Mere Christianity* (Westwood, New Jersey: Barbour and Company Inc., 1985), 45

8. HB, 92

9. HB, 100

10. HB, 94

11. HB, 97

12. HB, 99

13. HB, 100

14. Ibid.

15. Ibid.

16. David Scott, *A Revolution of Love: The Meaning of Mother Teresa* (Chicago: Loyola Press, 2005), 152

17. HB, 341

18. HB, 124

19. HB, 125

20. Ibid.

21. HB, 150

22. George A. Kilcourse, Jr., *Flannery O'Connor's Religious Imagination: A World with Everything Off Balance* (Mahwah, New Jersey: Paulist Press, 2001), 8

23. HB, 154

24. Ibid.

25. Kirsten Tagami, "Women of Letters," *The Atlanta Journal-Constitution,* May 10, 2007, A16

26. Flannery O'Connor, Letter to Betty Hester, October 31, 1956, Manuscript, Archives, and Rare Book Library, Emory University, Atlanta, Georgia

27. Ibid.

28. Kirsten Tagami, op.cit., A1

29. *The Catechism of the Catholic Church* (Vatican City: Libreria Editrice Vaticana, 1994), 566.

30. William Sessions in Kirsten Tagami, op. cit., A16

31. Bo Emerson, "Mystery Begins to Unravel," *The Atlanta Journal-Constitution*, March 1, 2009, H12
32. Flannery O'Connor, Letter to Betty Hester, October 31, 1956, Manuscript, Archives, and Rare Book Library, Emory University, Atlanta, Georgia
33. HB, 184. (The original of this letter, stored in the Emory University archives, is dated November 18.)
34. George A. Kilcourse, Jr., op. cit., 8
35. HB, 226
36. HB, 223
37. HB, 430
38. HB, 451
39. HB, 452
40. Ibid.
41. Ibid.
42. HB, 453
43. Ibid.
44. HB, 454
45. HB, 455
46. Ibid.
47. HB, 459
48. William Sessions, "Betty Hester: A Noble Soul" at www.2gcsu .edu/library/sc/collections/oconnor/hester.html
49. HB, 459
50. HB, 460
51. HB, 463
52. HB, 458
53. HB, 464
54. HB, 467
55. Flannery O'Connor, Letter to Betty Hester, March 24, 1962, Emory University, op. cit.
56. HB, 474
57. HB, 526
58. HB, 543
59. William Sessions, op. cit.
60. HB, 407

Chapter 4

1. HB, 97
2. Jean W. Cash, *Flannery O'Connor: A Life* (Knoxville: University of Tennessee Press, 2002), 247
3. HB, 476
4. Ibid.
5. Ibid.
6. HB, 477
7. Ibid.

8. Ibid.
9. HB, 478
10. HB, 479
11. Flannery O'Connor in *Collected Works*, op. cit., 1184
12. HB, 479
13. HB, 488
14. Ibid.
15. HB, 489
16. HB, 488
17. HB, 489
18. Ibid.
19. HB, 422
20. Ibid.
21. HB, 428
22. HB, 446
23. HB, 482
24. HB, 488
25. HB, 489
26. HB, 497
27. HB, 498
28. HB, 432
29. HB, 486
30. Jean W. Cash, op. cit., 248
31. James H. McCown, "Remembering Flannery O'Connor," *America*, September 8, 1979, 88
32. HB, 490
33. Ibid.

Chapter 5

1. HB, 145
2. Flannery O'Connor, Introduction to *A Memoir of Mary Ann* (Savannah: Frederic C. Beil, 1991), 10
3. Ibid., 11
4. HB, 394
5. Flannery O'Connor, Introduction to *A Memoir of Mary Ann*, op. cit., 4
6. HB, 394
7. Flannery O'Connor, Letter to Father J. H. McCown, May 4, 1959, Thomas F. Gossett papers, Rare Book, Manuscript, and Special Collections Library, Duke University, Durham, North Carolina
8. HB, 394
9. Flannery O'Connor, Introduction to *A Memoir of Mary Ann*, op. cit., 17
10. Ibid.
11. *Collected Works*, 1129

12. Flannery O'Connor, Introduction to *A Memoir of Mary Ann*, op. cit., 16
13. HB, 394
14. HB, 404
15. HB, 409
16. Flannery O'Connor, Introduction to *A Memoir of Mary Ann*, op. cit., 13–14
17. HB, 409
18. HB, 415
19. HB, 416
20. HB, 419
21. Ibid.
22. Flannery O'Connor, Introduction, op. cit., 18
23. Ibid., 15
24. Allen Pridgen, *Walker Percy's Sacramental Landscapes: The Search in the Desert* (Selinsgrove: Susquehanna University Press, 2000), 89
25. Gretchen Keiser, "Cancer Home Sisters Celebrate 50 Years of Service," *Georgia Bulletin*, April 20, 1989
26. Ibid.
27. Mother Anne Marie Holden, O. P., letter to author, July 11, 2007
28. Allen Pridgen, op. cit., 90
29. James H. McCown, "Remembering Flannery O'Connor," *America*, September 8, 1979, 88
30. HB, xii
31. Flannery O'Connor, Introduction, op. cit., 20
32. Joseph Cardinal Ratzinger, *God and the World: Believing and Living in Our Time – A Conversation with Peter Seewald* (San Francisco: Ignatius Press, 2002), 322
33. Flannery O'Connor, Introduction, op. cit., 20
34. Flannery O'Connor, Letter to Brainard Cheney, May 14, 1961, *The Correspondence of Flannery O'Connor and the Brainard Cheneys*, ed. C. Ralph Stephens (Jackson: University Press of Mississippi, 1986), 134
35. Flannery O'Connor, Introduction, op. cit., 9
36. Ibid., 19
37. Dominican Nuns of Our Lady of Perpetual Help Home, *A Memoir of Mary Ann* (Savannah: Frederic C. Beil, 1991), 122
38. HB, 577
39. Flannery O'Connor, introduction, op. cit., 14
40. HB, 423
41. Flannery O'Connor, Letter to Sister Evangelist, undated, archives, Dominican Sisters of Hawthorne, Rosary Hill Home, Hawthorne, New York
42. HB, 428
43. Ibid.
44. Ibid.
45. The Dominican Nuns, op. cit., 129

46. HB, 421
47. Flannery O'Connor, Letter to Sister Evangelist, April 17, 1961, archives Dominican Sisters of Hawthorne, op. cit.
48. HB, 430
49. HB, 430–431
50. Testimonials on cover of paperback edition of *A Memoir of Mary Ann* (New York: Dell Publishing Company, 1962)
51. HB, 445
52. Flannery O'Connor, Letter to Sister Josephine, September 24, 1961, archives, Dominican Sisters of Hawthorne, Rosary Hill Home, Hawthorne, New York
53. Flannery O'Connor, Letter to Sister Evangelist, November 11, 1961, ibid.
54. HB, 445
55. HB, 448
56. HB, 435
57. HB, 442

Chapter 6

1. HB, 176
2. HB, 114
3. Flannery O'Connor, "The Fiction Writer and His Country," *Mystery and Manners* (New York: Farrar, Straus, and Giroux, 1970), 27
4. HB, 180
5. HB, 143
6. HB, 204
7. HB, 221
8. HB, 161
9. HB, 215
10. HB, 183
11. Ibid.
12. Flannery O'Connor, "Writing Short Stories," *Mystery and Manners*, op. cit., 88
13. HB, 108
14. HB, 89
15. HB, 326
16. Flannery O'Connor, Letter to Betty Hester, March 7, 1958, Manuscript, Archives, and Rare Book Library, Emory University, Atlanta, Georgia
17. HB, 271
18. HB, 419
19. HB, 188
20. HB, 219
21. HB, 241
22. HB, 242

23. HB, 417
24. HB, 242
25. HB, 326
26. HB, 483
27. HB, 545
28. HB, 546
29. William Sessions, "Flannery O'Connor: A Memoir," *National Catholic Reporter*, October 28, 1964, Vol. 1, Issue 1, 9

Chapter 7

1. HB, 207
2. HB, 137
3. HB, 138
4. HB, 139
5. HB, 140
6. HB, 139
7. HB, 218
8. HB, 150
9. Flannery O'Connor, Letter to Leo J. Zuber, August 3, 1962, in Leo J. Zuber and Carter W. Martin, eds., *The Presence of Grace and Other Book Reviews by Flannery O'Connor* (Athens: University of Georgia Press, 1983), 145
10. HB, 179
11. HB, 211
12. HB, 213
13. HB, 211
14. HB, 214
15. Carter W. Martin, introduction, *The Presence of Grace and Other Book Reviews by Flannery O'Connor*, 4
16. Ibid., 5
17. Ibid., 125
18. Flannery O'Connor, Letter to A, August 24, 1956, *Collected Works* (New York: Library of America, 1988), 999
19. HB, 142
20. Ibid.
21. HB, 143
22. Ibid.
23. Ibid.
24. HB, 144
25. Flannery O'Connor, review of *The Malefactors*, *The Bulletin*, March 31, 1956, in *The Presence of Grace and Other Book Reviews by Flannery O'Connor*, op. cit., 15–16
26. Flannery O'Connor, Letter to Betty Hester, March 10, 1956, Manuscript, Archives, and Rare Book Library, Emory University, Atlanta, Georgia
27. HB, 272

28. Flannery O'Connor, Letter to Betty Hester, March 14, 1956, Manuscript, Archives, and Rare Book Library, Emory University, Atlanta, Georgia
29. Flannery O'Connor, *Collected Works*, 1130
30. HB, 497
31. HB, 506
32. Flannery O'Connor, Letter to Father Romagosa, May 4, 1959, in Sura P. Rath, "An Evolving Friendship: Flannery O'Connor's Correspondence with Father Edward J. Romagosa, S. J.," *Flannery O'Connor Bulletin*, Volume 17, 1988–1989, 2–3
33. Flannery O'Connor, Letter to Father Romagosa, January 25, 1960, in ibid., 3
34. Sura P. Rath, "An Evolving Friendship: Flannery O'Connor's Correspondence with Father Edward J. Romagosa, S. J.," op. cit., 4
35. John R. May, "Blue-Bleak Embers: The Letters of Flannery O'Connor and Youree Watson," *The New Orleans Review,* Volume 6.4, 1979, 337
36. Father Youree Watson, Letter to Flannery O'Connor, July 31, 1958 in John R. May, op. cit., 338–339
37. Flannery O'Connor, Letter to Father Youree Watson, January 17, 1960, in John R. May, op. cit., 341
38. Father Youree Watson, Letter to Flannery O'Connor, February 3, 1960, in John R. May, op. cit., 345
39. HB, 138
40. Flannery O'Connor, "Catholic Novelists," *Mystery and Manners*, op.cit., 171

Chapter 8

1. Flannery O'Connor, Letter to Betty Hester, September 5, 1959, Manuscript, Archives, and Rare Book Library, Emory University, Atlanta, Georgia
2. HB, 262
3. HB, 299
4. Flannery O'Connor, Letter to Betty Hester, May 19, 1956, Manuscript, Archives, and Rare Book Library, Emory University
5. HB, 131
6. Flannery O'Connor, "Catholic Novelists" in *Mystery and Manners*, op. cit., 175
7. HB, 192
8. HB, 357
9. HB, 248
10. James H. McCown, "Remembering Flannery O'Connor," *America*, September 8, 1979, 88

11. HB, 130. (Note: The original letter in the archives at Emory University is dated January 19, although *The Habit of Being* has it dated January 16.)
12. HB, 137. (Note: The actual title of her book is mentioned on page 133)
13. Flannery O'Connor, Letter to Father Romagosa, May 4, 1959, in Sura P. Rath, op. cit., 2
14. HB, 137
15. James H. McCown, op. cit., 86
16. Ibid., 87
17. HB, 137
18. James H. McCown, op. cit., 86
19. Ibid., 87
20. James H. McCown op. cit., 87
21. HB, 133
22. HB, 187
23. Flannery O'Connor, Letter to Father James H. McCown, January 12, 1958, in *Collected Works*, 1061
24. James H. McCown, op. cit., 88
25. Flannery O'Connor, Letter to Father J. H. McCown, Ground Hog Day, 1958, Thomas F. Gossett Collection, Rare Book, Manuscripts, and Special Collections Library, Duke University, Durham, North Carolina
26. HB, 462
27. HB, 141–142
28. HB, 318
29. HB, 327
30. Flannery O'Connor, Letter to Father James H. McCown, December 29, 1957, in *Collected Works,* 1057. (Note: This letter is dated December 20, 1957 in *The Habit of Being*, but the original letter in the archives at Duke University is dated December 29, 1957.)
31. Ibid., 1058
32. Flannery O'Connor, Letter to Leo J. Zuber, July 8, 1962, in *The Presence of Grace and Other Book Reviews by Flannery O'Connor*, ed. Leo J. Zuber and Carter W. Martin (Athens: University of Georgia Press, 1983), 144
33. Father J.H. McCown, op. cit., 88
34. HB, 263
35. HB, 262
36. HB, 259
37. HB, 263
38. HB, 365
39. Flannery O'Connor, Letter to Father J.H. McCown, January 7, 1960, Thomas F. Gossett Collection
40. HB, 309
41. Ibid.
42. HB, 366

43. HB, 468
44. James Hart McCown, *With Crooked Lines: Early Years of an Alabama Jesuit* (Mobile, Alabama: Spring Hill College Press, 1990), 130
45. Ibid.
46. HB, 347
47. HB, 179
48. HB, 155
49. HB, 307–308

Chapter 9

1. Paul Elie, *The Life You Save May Be Your Own: An American Pilgrimage* (New York: Farrar, Straus, and Giroux, 2003), 327
2. Ibid., 328
3. Sally Fitzgerald, HB, xviii
4. Ibid., xix
5. James Hart McCown, *With Crooked Lines: Early Years of an Alabama Jesuit* (Mobile, Alabama: Spring Hill College Press, 1990), 96
6. Ibid., 92
7. Ibid.
8. Ibid., 93
9. Ibid., 94
10. Flannery O'Connor, Letter to Brainard Cheney, October 12, 1958, in *The Correspondence of Flannery O'Connor and the Brainard Cheneys,* ed. C. Ralph Stephens (Jackson: University Press of Mississippi, 1986), 75
11. Brainard Cheney, Letter to Flannery O'Connor, October 22, 1958, in *The Correspondence of Flannery O'Connor and the Brainard Cheneys*, 76
12. Flannery O'Connor, Letter to Brainard Cheney, October 24, 1958, in Ibid., 77
13. Ibid., 78
14. HB, 204
15. HB, 246
16. Ralph C. Wood, *Flannery O'Connor and the Christ-Haunted South* (Grand Rapids, Michigan: Wm. B. Eerdmans Publishing Company, 2004), 100-101
17. Ibid., 98
18. HB, 193
19. HB, 194
20. HB, 195
21. HB, 201
22. Sarah Gordon and Craig Amason, *A Literary Guide to Flannery O'Connor's Georgia* (Athens: University of Georgia Press, 2008), 93
23. Flannery O'Connor, *Wise Blood* in *Collected Works*, 86

24. Flannery O'Connor, "The Displaced Person" in ibid., 297
25. HB, 329
26. Ralph C. Wood, op. cit., 112
27. Ibid., 102
28. HB, 475
29. Flannery O'Connor, Letter to Betty Hester, September 7, 1957, Manuscript, Archives, and Rare Book Library, Emory University, Atlanta, Georgia
30. HB, 253
31. Flannery O'Connor, Letter to Brainard Cheney, August 9, 1962, *The Correspondence of Flannery O'Connor and the Brainard Cheneys*, op. cit., 154
32. HB, 542
33. Flannery O'Connor, Letter to Brainard Cheney, April 10, 1960, *The Correspondence of Flannery O'Connor and the Brainard Cheneys*, op. cit., 115
34. HB, 580
35. Flannery O'Connor, "The Artificial Nigger" in *Collected Works*, 230
36. HB, 101
37. HB, 140
38. HB, 78
39. Flannery O'Connor in *Flannery O'Connor and the Christ-Haunted South,* op. cit., 103
40. Ralph C. Wood in ibid.
41. Sally Fitzgerald, HB, xviii
42. C. Ross Mullins, Jr., "Flannery O'Connor: An Interview" in *Conversations with Flannery O'Connor*, ed. Rosemary M. Magee (Jackson: University Press of Mississippi, 1987), 104
43. HB, 302

Chapter 10

1. Flannery O'Connor, Letter to Father Youree Watson, May 13, 1958, in John May, "Blue-Bleak Embers: The Letters of Flannery O'Connor and Youree Watson," *The New Orleans Review*, Volume 6.4, 1979, 338
2. HB, 250
3. HB, 231
4. HB, 250
5. Ibid.
6. Flannery O'Connor, Letter to Sally and Robert Fitzgerald, November 4, 1957, in *Collected Works*, op.cit., 1048
7. HB, 258
8. HB, 267–268
9. HB, 268
10. HB, 277

11. HB, 279
12. HB, 280
13. Flannery O'Connor, Letter to Betty Hester, May 17, 1958, Manuscripts, Archives, and Rare Book Library, Emory University
14. Flannery O'Connor, Letter to Father McCown, May 11, 1958, Thomas F. Gossett Collection, Rare Books, Manuscripts, and Special Collections Library, Duke University
15. HB, 285
16. HB, 280
17. HB, 286
18. Ibid.
19. William Sessions, "Flannery O'Connor: A Memoir," *National Catholic Reporter*, October 28, 1964, Volume 1, Issue 1, 9
20. HB, 282
21. Flannery O'Connor, Letter to Father Youree Watson, August 17, 1958, in "Blue-Bleak Embers," op. cit., 339
22. HB, 280
23. HB, 281
24. Flannery O'Connor, Letter to Betty Hester, May 31, 1958, Manuscripts, Archives, and Rare Book Library, Emory University
25. HB, 305
26. HB, 310
27. HB, 306
28. Flannery O'Connor, Letter to Father Youree Wason, August 17, 1958, in "Blue-Bleak Embers," op. cit., 339
29. HB, 316

Chapter 11

1. James H. McCown, "Remembering Flannery O'Connor," *America*, September 8, 1979, 86
2. HB, 61
3. HB, 562
4. HB, 56
5. Flannery O'Connor, Letter to A, December 11, 1956, *Collected Works*, op.cit., 1012
6. Flannery O'Connor, "Novelist and Believer," *Mystery and Manners*, selected and edited by Sally and Robert Fitzgerald (New York: Farrar, Straus, and Giroux, 1970), 157
7. HB, 104
8. HB, 29
9. HB, 91–92
10. HB, 84
11. HB, 26
12. HB, 28

13. Flannery O'Connor, letter to Brainard Cheney, May 11, 1956, in *The Correspondence of Flannery O'Connor and the Brainard Cheneys,* ed. C. Ralph Stephens (Jackson: University Press of Mississippi: 1986), 36

14. HB, 217

15. Flannery O'Connor, "The King of the Birds," *Mystery and Manners*, op. cit., 5

16. Ibid.

17. Sally Fitzgerald, quoted in "Author's Beloved Peacocks Come to Violent End," *The Post and Courier*, Charleston, South Carolina, November 29, 1991, 10-B

18. Flannery O'Connor, "The King of the Birds," *Mystery and Manners*, op. cit., 6

19. HB, 57

20. HB, 68

21. HB, 67

22. HB, 219

23. HB, 223

24. HB, 228

25. HB, 240

26. James H. McCown, op. cit., 88

27. Flannery O'Connor, "The King of the Birds," *Mystery and Manners*, op. cit., 10

28. Flannery O'Connor, "The Displaced Person," *Collected Works*, op. cit., 317

29. Flannery O'Connor, "The King of the Birds," op. cit., 10

30. HB, 167

31. HB, 154

32. HB, 528

33. Flannery O'Connor, Letter to Betty Hester, September 2, 1961, Manuscript, Archives, and Rare Books Library, Emory University, Atlanta, Georgia

34. Flannery O'Connor, Letter to Sister Julie, Sally Fitzgerald Collection, May 12, 1962, Manuscript, Archives, and Rare Books Library, Emory University, Atlanta, Georgia

35. Flannery O'Connor, Letter to Betty Hester, January 26, 1962, Manuscript, Archives, and Rare Books Library, Emory University, Atlanta, Georgia

36. HB, 502

37. Flannery O'Connor, Letter to Sister Julie, Sally Fitzgerald Collection, October 13, 1963, Manuscript, Archives, and Rare Books Library, Emory University, Atlanta, Georgia

38. HB, 475

39. HB, 545

40. HB, 482

41. Flannery O'Connor, Letter to Father Romagosa, S. J., in Sura P. Rath: "An Evolving Friendship: Flannery O'Connor's

Correspondence with Father Edward J. Romagosa, S. J.," *Flannery O'Connor Bulletin*, 17(1988–89), 6

42. HB, 555
43. HB, 574
44. HB, 587
45. Associated Press, "Author's Beloved Peacocks Meet a Violent End," op. cit., 10-B
46. HB, 218

Chapter 12

1. HB, 354
2. Robert Fitzgerald in Flannery O'Connor, *Everything That Rises Must Converge* (New York: Farrar, Straus and Giroux: 1965), xvii
3. HB, 22
4. Ibid.
5. HB, 24
6. HB, 53
7. Ibid.
8. Robert Ellsberg, *Flannery O'Connor: Spiritual Writings* (Maryknoll, New York: Orbis Books, 2003), 145
9. Robert Ellsberg, *The Saints' Guide to Happiness* (New York: Doubleday, 2003), 117
10. HB, 509
11. Sally Fitzgerald, "Chronology" in *Collected Works*, op.cit., 1246–1247
12. Jean W. Cash, *Flannery O'Connor: A Life*, op. cit., 138
13. HB, 55
14. HB, 57
15. HB, 67
16. Flannery O'Connor, Letter to Beverly Brunson, September 13, 1954, *Flannery O'Connor: Collected Works*, op.cit., 925
17. Flannery O'Connor, Letter to Beverly Brunson, January 1, 1955 in ibid., 928–929
18. Flannery O'Connor, Letter to Robert Lowell, March 26, 1954 in ibid., 924
19. HB, 346
20. HB, 336
21. HB, 458
22. HB, 500
23. HB, 275
24. Ibid.
25. HB, 104
26. HB, 107
27. Flannery O'Connor, letter to Fanny Cheney, September 29, 1955, in *The Correspondence of Flannery O'Connor and the Brainard*

Cheneys, ed. C. Ralph Stephens (Jackson: University Press of Mississippi, 1986), 23

28. HB, 107
29. HB, 116–117
30. HB, 151
31. HB, 168
32. HB, 266
33. HB, 163
34. Ibid.
35. Ibid.
36. Joseph Cardinal Ratzinger, *God and the World: Believing and Living in Our Time. A Conversation with Peter Seewald* (San Francisco: Ignatius Press, 2002), 433–434
37. HB, 420
38. HB, 421
39. HB, 422
40. HB, 423
41. Ibid.
42. Flannery O'Connor, Letter to Father Youree Watson, December 25, 1960, in John R. May, ed., "Blue-Bleak Embers: The Letters of Flannery O'Connor and Youree Watson," *The New Orleans Review*, Volume 6.4, 1979, 350
43. Ibid., 351
44. Ibid.
45. Flannery O'Connor, Letter to Father McCown, June 23, 1961, Thomas F. Gossett collection, Rare Book, Manuscripts, and Special Collections Library, Duke University, Durham, North Carolina
46. Flannery O'Connor, Letter to Father McCown, August 2, 1961 in ibid
47. HB, 527
48. Thomas F. Gossett, "Flannery O'Connor's Humor with a Serious Purpose, *Studies in American Humor*, Volume 3, Number 3, January 1977, 178
49. Thérèse of Lisieux *in The Autobiography of Saint Thérèse of Lisieux: The Story of a Soul*, trans. John Beevers (New York: Doubleday, 1957), 91
50. Thérèse of Lisieux in André Combs, *The Spirituality of St. Thérèse: An Introduction* (New York: P. J. Kenedy and Sons, 1950), 148–150
51. Columba Downey, ed., *The Little Flower Prayer Book: A Carmelite Manual of Prayer*, (Chicago: Carmelite Press, 1926), 139
52. HB, 523
53. HB, 542
54. HB, 554
55. HB, 555
56. Flannery O'Connor, Letter to Father McCown, February 20, 1964, Thomas F. Gossett collection, op. cit

57. HB, 570

58. HB, 559

59. Youree Watson, Letter to Flannery O'Connor, March 12, 1964, in John R. May, ed. "Blue-Bleak Embers," op. cit., 355

60. Flannery O'Connor, letter to Youree Watson, March 15, 1964, in ibid., 356

61. Sally Fitzgerald, "Chronology" in *Collected Works*, op. cit., 1256

62. HB, 574

63. HB 582–583

64. HB, 583

65. William Sessions, "Flannery O'Connor: A Memoir," op. cit., 9

66. HB, 591

67. HB, 596

68. Archbishop Paul J. Hallinan, "Archbishop's Notebook," *The Georgia Bulletin*, August 6, 1964

69. Flannery O'Connor, Letter to Father Romagosa, April 11, 1964 in Sura P. Rath, "An Evolving Friendship: Flannery O'Connor's Correspondence with Father Edward J. Romagosa, S. J.," Flannery O'Connor Bulletin, 17 (1988-1989), 6

70. Thérèse of Lisieux, *The Autobiography of Saint Thérèse of Lisieux: The Story of a Soul*, op.cit., 113